THE
CHICKASAW

ILLINOIS

MISSOURI

KENTUCKY

WEST
VIRGINIA

VIRGINIA

ARKANSAS

TENNESSEE

Arkansas

Cherokee

NORTH
CAROLINA

River

Quapaw

River

CHICKASAW

Tennessee

River

SOUTH
CAROLINA

Mississippi

Creek

Tunica

MISSISSIPPI

ALABAMA

GEORGIA

Choctaw

Natchez

LOUISIANA

FLORIDA

GULF OF MEXICO

THE
CHICKASAW

Duane K. Hale
University of Oklahoma

Arrell M. Gibson
University of Oklahoma

Frank W. Porter III
General Editor

CHELSEA HOUSE PUBLISHERS
New York   Philadelphia

On the cover Two Chickasaw toli sticks made in the late 19th century. Each consists of a rawhide net attached to a wooden handle.

Chelsea House Publishers
Editor-in-Chief Remmel Nunn
Managing Editor Karyn Gullen Browne
Copy Chief Juliann Barbato
Picture Editor Adrian G. Allen
Art Director Maria Epes
Deputy Copy Chief Mark Rifkin
Assistant Art Director Loraine Machlin
Manufacturing Manager Gerald Levine
Production Manager Joseph Romano
Production Coordinator Marie Claire Cebrián

Indians of North America
Senior Editor Liz Sonneborn

Staff for **THE CHICKASAW**
Copy Editor Philip Koslow
Editorial Assistant Nicole Claro
Designer Debora Smith
Picture Researcher Sandy Jones

First Printing

1 3 5 7 9 8 6 4 2

Library of Congress Cataloging-in-Publication Data

Hale, Duane K.
The Chickasaw/by Duane K. Hale and Arrell M. Gibson.
p. cm.—(Indians of North America)
Includes bibliographical references.
Summary: Examines the history, changing fortunes, and current situation of the Chickasaw Indians. Includes a photo essay on their crafts.
ISBN 1-55546-697-4
    0-7910-0372-8 (pbk.)
1. Chickasaw Indians. [1. Chickasaw Indians. 2. Indians of North America.] I. Gibson, Arrell Morgan. II. Title III. Series: Indians of North America (Chelsea House Publishers)   90-34775
E99.C55H35 1990   CIP
973'.04973—dc20   AC

CONTENTS

INDIANS OF NORTH AMERICA

CHELSEA HOUSE PUBLISHERS

INDIANS OF NORTH AMERICA: CONFLICT AND SURVIVAL

Frank W. Porter III

The Indians survived our open intention of wiping them out, and since the tide turned they have even weathered our good intentions toward them, which can be much more deadly.

John Steinbeck
America and Americans

When Europeans first reached the North American continent, they found hundreds of tribes occupying a vast and rich country. The newcomers quickly recognized the wealth of natural resources. They were not, however, so quick or willing to recognize the spiritual, cultural, and intellectual riches of the people they called Indians.

The Indians of North America examines the problems that develop when people with different cultures come together. For American Indians, the consequences of their interaction with non-Indian people have been both productive and tragic. The Europeans believed they had "discovered" a "New World," but their religious bigotry, cultural bias, and materialistic world view kept them from appreciating and understanding the people who lived in it. All too often they attempted to change the way of life of the indigenous people. The Spanish conquistadores wanted the Indians as a source of labor. The Christian missionaries, many of whom were English, viewed them as potential converts. French traders and trappers used the Indians as a means to obtain pelts. As Francis Parkman, the 19th-century historian, stated, "Spanish civilization crushed the Indian; English civilization scorned and neglected him; French civilization embraced and cherished him."

Nearly 500 years later, many people think of American Indians as curious vestiges of a distant past, waging a futile war to survive in a Space Age society. Even today, our understanding of the history and culture of American Indians is too often derived from unsympathetic, culturally biased, and in-accurate reports. The American Indian, described and portrayed in thousands of movies, television programs, books, articles, and government studies, has either been raised to the status of the "noble savage" or disparaged as the "wild Indian" who resisted the westward expansion of the American frontier.

Where in this popular view are the real Indians, the human beings and communities whose ancestors can be traced back to ice-age hunters? Where are the creative and indomitable people whose sophisticated technologies used the natural resources to ensure their survival, whose military skill might even have prevented European settlement of North America if not for dev-astating epidemics and disruption of the ecology? Where are the men and women who are today diligently struggling to assert their legal rights and express once again the value of their heritage?

The various Indian tribes of North America, like people everywhere, have a history that includes population expansion, adaptation to a range of regional environments, trade across wide networks, internal strife, and warfare. This was the reality. Europeans justified their conquests, however, by creating a mythical image of the New World and its native people. In this myth, the New World was a virgin land, waiting for the Europeans. The arrival of Christopher Columbus ended a timeless primitiveness for the original in-habitants.

Also part of this myth was the debate over the origins of the American Indians. Fantastic and diverse answers were proposed by the early explorers, missionairies, and settlers. Some thought that the Indians were descended from the Ten Lost Tribes of Israel, others that they were descended from inhabitants of the lost continent of Atlantis. One writer suggested that the Indians had reached North America in another Noah's ark.

A later myth, perpetrated by many historians, focused on the relentless persecution during the past five centuries until only a scattering of these "primitive" people remained to be herded onto reservations. This view fails to chronicle the overt and covert ways in which the Indians successfully coped with the intruders.

All of these myths presented one-sided interpretations that ignored the complexity of European and American events and policies. All left serious questions unanswered. What were the origins of the American Indians? Where did they come from? How and when did they get to the New World? What was their life—their culture—really like?

In the late 1800s, anthropologists and archaeologists in the Smithsonian Institution's newly created Bureau of American Ethnology in Washington,

D.C., began to study scientifically the history and culture of the Indians of North America. They were motivated by an honest belief that the Indians were on the verge of extinction and that along with them would vanish their languages, religious beliefs, technology, myths, and legends. These men and women went out to visit, study, and record data from as many Indian communities as possible before this information was forever lost.

By this time there was a new myth in the national consciousness. American Indians existed as figures in the American past. They had performed a historical mission. They had challenged white settlers who trekked across the continent. Once conquered, however, they were supposed to accept graciously the way of life of their conquerors.

The reality again was different. American Indians resisted both actively and passively. They refused to lose their unique identity, to be assimilated into white society. Many whites viewed the Indians not only as members of a conquered nation but also as "inferior" and "unequal." The rights of the Indians could be expanded, contracted, or modified as the conquerors saw fit. In every generation, white society asked itself what to do with the American Indians. Their answers have resulted in the twists and turns of federal Indian policy.

There were two general approaches. One way was to raise the Indians to a "higher level" by "civilizing" them. Zealous missionaries considered it their Christian duty to elevate the Indian through conversion and scanty education. The other approach was to ignore the Indians until they disappeared under pressure from the ever-expanding white society. The myth of the "vanishing Indian" gave stronger support to the latter option, helping to justify the taking of the Indians' land.

Prior to the end of the 18th century, there was no national policy on Indians simply because the American nation has not yet come into existence. American Indians similarly did not possess a political or social unity with which to confront the various Europeans. They were not homogeneous. Rather, they were loosely formed bands and tribes, speaking nearly 300 languages and thousands of dialects. The collective identity felt by Indians today is a result of their common experiences of defeat and/or mistreatment at the hands of whites.

During the colonial period, the British crown did not have a coordinated policy toward the Indians of North America. Specific tribes (most notably the Iroquois and the Cherokee) became military and political pawns used by both the crown and the individual colonies. The success of the American Revolution brought no immediate change. When the United States acquired new territory from France and Mexico in the early 19th century, the federal government wanted to open this land to settlement by homesteaders. But the Indian tribes that lived on this land had signed treaties with European governments assuring their title to the land. Now the United States assumed legal responsibility for honoring these treaties.

At first, President Thomas Jefferson believed that the Louisiana Purchase contained sufficient land for both the Indians and the white population. Within a generation, though, it became clear that the Indians would not be allowed to remain. In the 1830s the federal government began to coerce the eastern tribes to sign treaties agreeing to relinquish their ancestral land and move west of the Mississippi River. Whenever these negotiations failed, President Andrew Jackson used the military to remove the Indians. The southeastern tribes, promised food and transportation during their removal to the West, were instead forced to walk the "Trail of Tears." More than 4,000 men, woman, and children died during this forced march. The "removal policy" was successful in opening the land to homesteaders, but it created enormous hardships for the Indians.

By 1871 most of the tribes in the United States had signed treaties ceding most or all of their ancestral land in exchange for reservations and welfare. The treaty terms were intended to bind both parties for all time. But in the General Allotment Act of 1887, the federal government changed its policy again. Now the goal was to make tribal members into individual landowners and farmers, encouraging their absorption into white society. This policy was advantageous to whites who were eager to acquire Indian land, but it proved disastrous for the Indians. One hundred thirty-eight million acres of reservation land were subdivided into tracts of 160, 80, or as little as 40 acres, and allotted tribe members on an individual basis. Land owned in this way was said to have "trust status" and could not be sold. But the surplus land—all Indian land not allotted to individuals—was opened (for sale) to white settlers. Ultimately, more than 90 million acres of land were taken from the Indians by legal and illegal means.

The resulting loss of land was a catastrophe for the Indians. It was necessary to make it illegal for Indians to sell their land to non-Indians. The Indian Reorganization Act of 1934 officially ended the allotment period. Tribes that voted to accept the provisions of this act were reorganized, and an effort was made to purchase land within preexisting reservations to restore an adequate land base.

Ten years later, in 1944, federal Indian policy again shifted. Now the federal government wanted to get out of the "Indian business." In 1953 an act of Congress named specific tribes whose trust status was to be ended "at the earliest possible time." This new law enabled the United States to end unilaterally, whether the Indians wished it or not, the special status that protected the land in Indian tribal reservations. In the 1950s federal Indian policy was to transfer federal responsibility and jurisdiction to state governments, encourage the physical relocation of Indian peoples from reservations to urban areas, and hasten the termination, or extinction, of tribes.

Between 1954 and 1962 Congress passed specific laws authorizing the termination of more than 100 tribal groups. The stated purpose of the termination policy was to ensure the full and complete integration of Indians into American society. However, there is a less benign way to interpret this legislation. Even as termination was being discussed in Congress, 133 separate bills were introduced to permit the transfer of trust land ownership from Indians to non-Indians.

With the Johnson administration in the 1960s the federal government began to reject termination. In the 1970s yet another Indian policy emerged. Known as "self-determination," it favored keeping the protective role of the federal government while increasing tribal participation in, and control of, important areas of local government. In 1983 President Reagan, in a policy statement on Indian affairs, restated the unique "government is government" relationship of the United States with the Indians. However, federal programs since then have moved toward transferring Indian affairs to individual states, which have long desired to gain control of Indian land and resources.

As long as American Indians retain power, land, and resources that are coveted by the states and the federal government, there will continue to be a "clash of cultures," and the issues will be contested in the courts, Congress, the White House, and even in the international human rights community. To give all Americans a greater comprehension of the issues and conflicts involving American Indians today is a major goal of this series. These issues are not easily understood, nor can these conflicts be readily resolved. The study of North American Indian history and culture is a necessary and important step toward that comprehension. All Americans must learn the history of the relations between the Indians and the federal government, recognize the unique legal status of the Indians, and understand the heritage and cultures of the Indians of North America.

A detail from a 1980 painting by the Chickasaw artist Martha Ann Sheffield, showing a Chickasaw woman cooking outside her family's winter house. This work is one of a series of paintings done by Sheffield between 1975 and 1980 that depict scenes of traditional Chickasaw society and tribal history. The series now hangs in the Chickasaw Community Center in Ada, Oklahoma.

CHICSA'S PEOPLE

Long ago, a great people lived in a dark, forbidding land in the distant west. One day their god, Ababinili, directed the elders and holy men to leave that land and lead their people in search of a new home in the bright domain situated toward the rising sun.

Their travels were guided by a sacred staff. At the end of each day's journey through the wilderness, the holy men placed the pole upright in the ground. During the night, the staff was stirred by cosmic forces. The direction it assumed at dawn dictated the course of the next day's march. Almost without fail, the staff commanded the travelers to move eastward.

At one location, the people came upon a raging flood, so they constructed rafts in order to continue their journey. Soon, a raven holding an ear of corn appeared to them. Speaking through the holy men, Ababinili told the people to save the corn and plant it in their new land. After many days, the wanderers crossed a great river. The next morning, they found that the sacred staff stood erect, unmoved from the position in which the holy men had placed it the night before. At last, the people had arrived in their eastern home.

Two leaders, Chacta and Chicsa, decided that the people should split into two groups and settle in adjacent territories. Chacta led his group south. These people became known as the Choctaw. Chicsa settled his followers to the north. They were thereafter referred to as the Chickasaw.

This story of the formation of the Chickasaw, a large Indian tribe that traditionally lived in what are now the Tombigbee Highlands of northern Mississippi, has long been passed on from generation to generation. As in the past, repeating this and other tribal legends is one means by which the Chickasaw Indians now teach their children about their ethnic heritage. Centuries have passed since their ancestors were led to their southeastern homeland by Ababinili, and in that time many elements of the Chickasaw's traditional culture have been forever lost. But throughout the tribe's history, the Indians' great pride in their Chickasaw identity has remained unchanged.

Information about the ancient Chickasaw way of life comes from three sources—the tribe's traditional stories, such as the legend of their migration east; artifacts, such as tools and ornaments, made by the early Chickasaw; and chronicles written by the European explorers who began arriving in the Chickasaw homeland in the 16th century. These sources combine to create a picture of a powerful tribe that courageously dominated the military, diplomatic, and commercial life of the lower Mississippi River valley for hundreds of years.

Prehistorians have found evidence that confirms several points of the Chickasaw's story of their origins. At one time, the Chickasaw and the Choctaw were probably one people who migrated eastward to what is now the American Southeast. In the region, their population grew, and they divided into two tribes. The great similarities between the Chickasaw's and Choctaw's native religion, social organization, tribal government, marriage

and family customs, and other practices support this theory. Likewise, the basic similarity (despite minor differences) between the Chickasaw and Choctaw languages also suggests that these groups are closely related. Their languages are categorized by linguists as part of the Muskogean language family. The Creek, one of the Chickasaw's other traditional neighbors, also spoke Muskogean languages and shared many cultural traits with the Chickasaw.

According to early European documents, the Chickasaw numbered about 5,000. Although not as populous as the Choctaw (22,000), the Creek (26,000), or the Cherokee (23,000) to the east, the Chickasaw ruled over a large territory. By the 16th century, the tribe had established towns in present-day northern Mississippi and northeastern Alabama but also controlled additional lands extending to central Kentucky and Tennessee. This fringe territory, which the Chickasaw used as hunting grounds, had been obtained by conquest. Fierce in combat, the Chickasaw were described by European visitors as being as brave as lions on the battlefield.

Before the arrival of Europeans, the abundant resources of the Chickasaw's vast domain provided the people with everything they needed to survive. Much of their food was obtained by hunting animals, especially deer and bears. Chickasaw hunters were skilled in tracking, trapping, and using decoys

Arrow points that were unearthed in the traditional Chickasaw domain. Analyzing artifacts such as these provides prehistorians with much of their knowledge of early Chickasaw culture.

and calls to attract their prey, which they usually killed using bows and arrows with points crafted from deer antlers. The year's longest hunt occurred in autumn.

Most of a hunter's catch was consumed by the members of his household, but he often contributed a portion of it to a public feast or gave meat to elderly people living in his town. The Chickasaw ate meat fresh or dried and smoked it for later use. By heating bear fat, they obtained a sweet, digestible oil that they used in cooking and rubbed on their hair for protection from the elements.

The many creeks and rivers of the Chickasaw domain supplied the tribespeople with a variety of fish. Chickasaw fishermen collected and pulverized wild plants, such as devil's shoestring, and nuts, such as buckeyes and walnuts, to create natural poisons, which they cast into deep holes in streams near their homes. These poisons stunned fish but were harmless to humans. When drugged catfish, drum, perch, bass, and suckers rose to the surface of the water, the fishermen could easily catch them by grabbing them, spearing them, or shooting them with an arrow fitted with a special barb and line, with which they could pull the pierced fish from the water. The Chickasaw also used nets woven from deer sinew to trap fish.

Another major component of the Chickasaw's food supply was the crops they farmed. Most of the work in the fields was performed by women and children, assisted by Indian slaves captured from other tribes by Chickasaw war parties. In early times, corn was the principal food crop, although the Chickasaw also raised sunflowers, peas, beans, squash, pumpkins, tobacco, and melons.

Chickasaw women and children were also responsible for gathering wild plant foods in season. Among these were wild onions, grapes, plums, persimmons, mulberries, strawberries, and hickory nuts. The Chickasaw made prunes and raisins by drying plums and grapes and pressed persimmons into cakes. They also boiled sassafras roots to make tea, seasoned their food with salt from local springs, and sweetened some dishes with honey.

In addition to food, the Chickasaw's environment provided them with everything they needed to make the ob-

jects they used in everyday life. These items included clay pots for cooking and for storing food and water; baskets woven from cane; mats woven from tree bark; and decorative mantles made from eagle, hawk, or swan feathers.

One of the most important natural resources of the Chickasaw domain was the dense forests, from which the Indians obtained home-building materials. Each Chickasaw household had two dwellings, one used in winter and one used in summer. The winter houses had a circular frame, about 25 feet in diameter, made of pine logs and poles tied together with bark thongs. Long blades of dry grass were used to make the roof, and a plaster of clay and dry grass formed the walls. Summer houses were rectangular and had gabled roofs. The wooden frames were covered with mats of bark or grass, which were woven loosely enough to allow air to circulate, helping the Chickasaw keep cool during the hot summer months. Lining the interior walls of their houses were beds made of long poles covered with mats or animal skins. Other furniture included small wooden seats and stools.

The Chickasaw also used logs to make pirogues, or dugout canoes. To create one of these boats, the Indians cut down a huge tree, burned the inside of its thick trunk, and scraped out the charred wood with clamshells. Chickasaw traders navigated their pirogues through the waterways of the lower Mississippi Valley in order to travel to markets in neighboring tribes' territory.

There they traded animal skins and hides and jars of bear's oil for such valued goods as conch shells, which the Chickasaw used in ceremonies, and pearls and sheet copper, from which they fashioned ornaments.

Chickasaw women made their family's clothing from animal skins and hides. In the summer, men dressed in deerskin breechcloths and shirts. Women wore dresses made from deerskins sewed together with fishbone needles threaded with deer sinews. In the winter, men put on long coats of panther, deer, bear, and otter skins with the flesh side out, and women wrapped themselves in soft buffalo calfskins. Women made footwear for the members of their family from deer-, elk, and bear skins, which the Indians tanned and softened by rubbing them with deer brains. When hunting, men wore special thigh-high boots to protect their legs from brambles and thorny thickets.

Politically, the Chickasaw nation

A detail from a Sheffield painting of a Chickasaw war party navigating the Mississippi River in large canoes. The tribe's military strength helped them control an enormous expanse of land in what is now Mississippi, Tennessee, and Alabama.

was divided into two large divisions—Impsaktca and Intcukwalipa. Both were further divided into clans, or groups of blood-related families. Each clan was governed by a council of elders and a clan *minko*, or chief, who was selected by the clan council. Throughout history, the number of clans in both divisions has varied from 7 to 15.

All clans were bound together in a loose confederation. This was ruled by the Chickasaw's principal chief, the high minko, who always came from the Impsaktca division. He was assisted in carrying out his duties by the *tishu minko*. Sharing power with these officials was the national council. Its members were clan minkos and several wise elders. When the high minko called a meeting of the national council, the tishu minko sent messengers to all Chickasaw towns to tell clan representatives to come to a special structure used only for national council meetings. There the councilmen would discuss military matters and other business of national interest.

The national council was responsible for making Chickasaw law, which was enforced locally by clan courts presided over by tribal elders. The laws regulated personal behavior and the duties and responsibilities of citizens. All Chickasaw were required to assist in the erection of town palisades and public buildings, such as council houses and religious shrines. The laws also monitored individuals' use of tribal land. The Chickasaw believed that land was a gift from their creator and thus could not be held as personal property. The people of each town instead shared common fields, which they cultivated together. In public granaries, they stored their harvest for distribution in time of need. Although private land ownership was not permissible under Chickasaw law, families could select specific plots to farm for their own subsistence. A local council of elders served as an arbitration court to settle any disputes between families over use of such tracts.

According to clan law, a husband and wife had to belong to different clans. When a man and woman wished to marry, the man sent his intended bride a small present. If she accepted this gift, they were considered engaged. The couple later married in a simple ceremony attended by clan elders and family members. During the marriage ceremony, the groom presented the bride with an ear of corn. She then responded by offering him a token of cakes made from cornmeal.

Clan membership was inherited from a person's mother. Therefore, children were always of a different clan from their father. A person's clan affiliation was so important that children had to be raised by members of their own clan. Youngsters were cared for by their mother and her brothers, whereas their father was responsible for the upbringing of his sister's children. Tribal elders also served as teachers for Chickasaw boys and girls, instructing them in the basic skills they would need to perform their adult future roles. Elders

A 1979 painting by Sheffield of a Chickasaw town as it probably looked before the arrival of Europeans in tribal territory in the mid-16th century.

also taught children about their tribal heritage by telling them age-old folktales that included important messages about Chickasaw tradition.

The Chickasaw were a deeply religious people whose beliefs were closely tied to the natural world. Their religion explained the many mysteries in their universe. For instance, they believed that lightning, thunder, and storms were expressions of Ababinili's anger or displeasure.

Ababinili was thought to have created all people out of dust. The Chickasaw believed the sun to be a manifestation of the supreme being's great power. A sacred fire was kept lit in each town as a symbol of the holy fire in the sky. Other Chickasaw deities included the Hottuk Ishtohoollo, who were good spirits, and Hottuk Ookproose, who were evil.

The tribe believed some supernatural beings lived among them on earth. For example, Lofas were 10-foot-tall giants who were said to hide game from hunters and cause disaster. More helpful creatures were the three-foot-tall Iyaganashas. They were said to teach hunters to stalk animals and to train the *aliktce*, healers charged with curing the sick. People with minor health problems were generally treated by female family members with teas and potions made from wild plants. But the Chickasaw believed that the seriously ill could only be healed by the special knowledge that the aliktce obtained from the Iyaganashas.

The Chickasaw performed communal rituals to win the favor of Ababinili, the sun force, and other deities. These religious activities were directed by two holy men called the *hopoye*. Each of the hopoye represented one of the two grand divisions of the Chickasaw. Lesser priests assisted the hopoye in performing their duties. These responsibilities included presiding over tribal ceremonies and supervising the people's observances of the laws of their creator. The hopoye also advised tribal leaders on political matters.

The Chickasaw's most important ritual was the Busk Festival, which was held in the spring after their corn crop ripened. The four-day observance began with the hopoye and their assistants extinguishing the community's sacred fire. After removing its ashes, the holy men used the powerful rays of the sun to start a new fire. Before the ceremony, Chickasaw women put out the cooking fires in their houses. Once the new sacred flame was lit, they carried blessed coals from it to renew their household fires. Thereby they symbolically brought the sun—the center of power in the Chickasaw's spiritual universe—into their own homes.

For the next two days of the Busk Festival, the worshipers ate no food. They finally broke their fast by drinking boiled snakeroot. This caused them to vomit, which the Chickasaw believed purged all evil from the body. The participants then feasted on roasted ears of corn.

In addition to purifying individuals, the Busk Festival symbolically renewed the Chickasaw Nation as a whole. During the ritual, outstanding warriors were honored, criminals (except murderers) were pardoned, and parents

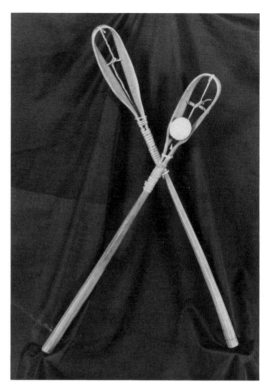

Two sticks and a ball used to play toli. *Similar to the modern-day game of lacrosse, toli was traditionally one of the Chickasaw's favorite forms of entertainment.*

were reminded by clan elders of their duty to instruct their young charges in tribal tradition.

The Busk Festival was not just a time for serious matters. Games, such as *toli, chunkey,* and *akabatle,* were also part of the springtime ritual. All of these were played on a rectangular court about 500 feet long. Toli was similar to the modern-day lacrosse, except that each player carried two sticks rather than one. The game of chunkey began with a special rounded stone being tossed onto the court. As it rolled, the players threw lances at it. The winner was the person whose lance struck closest to the place where the stone finally came to rest. Unlike toli and chunkey, which were played only by men, akabatle pitted a team of women against a team of men. The players gathered around a staff placed in the center of the court and tried to throw a ball so that it struck an effigy atop the pole. Before each contest, the hopoye performed a blessing and the people who had gathered for the game danced and sang, accompanied by music played on rattles, drums, and flutes. Following the game, the players and spectators enjoyed great feasts.

Another important Chickasaw ritual was the *picofa* ceremony. Presided over by one of the aliktce, it was performed to treat a seriously ill patient. The aliktce spent the first three days of the ceremony giving the patient emetics and potions. Members of the ill person's clan then came to the patient's dwelling and danced and sang. The Chickasaw believed a person became sick only if an animal spirit had entered his or her body. The picofa dance was a prayer to the various animal spirits asking for help for the afflicted. The lead dancer wore feathers or a skin from the particular animal thought to be responsible for the sickness. The dance concluded at dawn, when the aliktce announced that the spirit had left the patient's body and entered another animal. The ritual participants then held a feast in celebration.

In order to ensure support from their deities, the Chickasaw also performed rituals before going to war. Warriors first fasted for three days and nights. An elderly minko or distinguished warrior then gave a speech to rally the fighters. He explained his past exploits as a warrior and urged his listeners to match his courage and cunning in the battles to follow. The ceremony concluded with a dance performed by the warriors. If the war party returned victorious, a ceremony was held, during which the fighters displayed the scalps of their slain enemies and paraded the captives they had taken.

In the centuries following their arrival in the Southeast, the Chickasaw people developed into a great tribal power. A great variety of forces bound them together. Among these were their tight social organization, their tribal government and laws, their pride in tribal tradition, and their religious beliefs. That these cultural characteristics were the root of the Chickasaw's strength was quickly recognized by early European explorers. They and the non-Indians who later followed them to Chickasaw territory came to understand that undermining the Chickasaw's traditions was the first step toward seizing control of the tribal domain. From the tribe's first contact with whites, the history of the Chickasaw people would therefore become the story of their battle to retain what they could of the world their ancestors had created. ▲

An engraving of the head of a Chickasaw man, which appeared in A Concise Natural History of East and West Florida, *published in 1775.*

COLONIAL FRIENDS
AND
ENEMIES

In 1540, the Chickasaw met Europeans for the first time, an event that would change the Indians' life forever. Two years before, a Spanish force headed by explorer Hernando de Soto had sailed from Europe toward North America in search of riches. In May 1539, they landed on what is now the coast of Florida, just south of Tampa Bay. From there, the expedition proceeded to travel through the present-day states of Georgia, South and North Carolina, and Tennessee, enslaving or killing many of the Indians they encountered. By December 1540, the Spaniards reached the upper waters of the Tombigbee River in what is now Alabama. The chroniclers of the expedition called this land the Province of Chicaza.

As de Soto and his men crossed the Tombigbee, Chickasaw warriors tried to stop the curious invaders with a volley of arrows. When the Spaniards reached the river's west bank, they captured a number of Chickasaw hostages and demanded to see their chiefs. Chickasaw leaders and their attendants came quickly, bearing skins, shawls, food, and other gifts for the Europeans. De Soto insisted that the leaders provide his men and livestock with shelter and food to last the winter. As the days passed, the Indians and the Spaniards had uneasy, but increasingly regular, contact with each other.

By early March 1541, de Soto declared that he was ready to resume his march. He called the Chickasaw chiefs together and commanded that they surrender 200 warriors to him to carry his men's baggage. Tired of the hostile visitors and their unrelenting demands, a group of warriors slipped into the Spanish compound that night. Several men carried hot coals in small clay pots. With these, they ignited the crude barracks, and soon the Spanish camp was in flames. Chickasaw bowmen shot at the soldiers and their animals as they fled, killing 12 Spaniards and 57 horses. The survivors took refuge in a small village several miles away. While these soldiers were preparing to leave the area, the Chickasaw struck again. This time, de Soto's men repulsed their attackers. By April 26, 1541, the expedition had left the Province of Chicaza for good.

Following de Soto's departure, the Chickasaw would not encounter Europeans again for almost 150 years. During the Spanish expedition's four months' residence among them, the Chickasaw had learned something of European ways and goods, but this knowledge had little lasting impact on the tribe.

Through contact with other Indians, however, the Chickasaw heard more of their former acquaintances. They found out that other Spaniards had arrived in North America and were exploring lands to the southwest and southeast. The Chickasaw also learned of other European newcomers, the French and the British. These foreigners had established settlements far away—the French in present-day Canada and the British on the Atlantic coast—but were said to be trading, settling, and staging battles ever closer to the Chickasaw domain.

The French were the first Europeans to resume direct contact with the tribe. In 1673, an exploratory party led by Jacques Marquette and Louis Jolliet passed through Chickasaw territory as it traveled down the Mississippi River from Canada. Nine years later, an expedition of 55 Frenchmen and Indians, headed by René-Robert Cavelier, Sieur de La Salle, again sailed down the Mississippi en route to the Gulf of Mexico. On the western border of Chickasaw territory, La Salle's men erected a stockade to use as a base for search parties looking for a lost expedition member. In the course of their search, the Frenchmen met two Chickasaw Indians. La Salle gave them gifts as a peace offering but proceeded to the gulf before he and the Chickasaw could have any more extended contact.

Although the La Salle expedition itself had limited impact on the tribe, the Frenchmen's appearance in the lower Mississippi Valley signaled a new era for the region. Information obtained from the early French explorers made France determined to gain control of the area's vast resources and of the Mississippi, which provided a convenient water route between the Gulf of Mexico and France's northern colonial settlements. French officials recognized that they had to act quickly to establish a presence in the area because large numbers of British traders from the coast had already begun to move westward.

In 1698, two British traders, Thomas Welch and Anthony Dodsworth, arrived in the Chickasaw towns along the Tombigbee. They led horse trains packed with European goods that the Indians had never before seen, including cloth, guns, gunpowder, beads, knives, hatchets, hoes, scissors, axes,

A 19th-century engraving of the explorers Jacques Marquette and Louis Jolliet traveling down the Mississippi River in 1673. The members of this expedition were the first Frenchmen to enter Chickasaw territory.

brass wire, and brass kettles. The Indians were eager to trade for these items. Women wanted the hoes to farm their cornfields, the axes to chop firewood, and the cloth to make comfortable, decorative clothing for their family. Men prized the metal guns, knives, and hatchets, which were more successful on the hunt and deadlier on the battlefield than their handmade weapons. They also treasured brass wire as material for making arm and ankle bracelets and earrings. In return for these goods, the Chickasaw gave Welch and Dodsworth deerskins and Indian captives from other tribes. The traders shackled these captives and marched them eastward to the colony of Carolina, where they were sold to local plantation owners or shipped to slave markets in the West Indies.

Hoping to thwart the growing economic relationship between the British and the Chickasaw and other area tribes, the French in 1699 established a post, Fort Biloxi, on the Gulf of Mexico, south of Chickasaw territory. Other French settlements were soon founded on the gulf under the direction of explorer Pierre Le Moyne, Sieur d'Iberville. Among these settlements was Mobile, which became the administrative center of the French province of Louisiana, the name used by La Salle to designate all the land watered by the Mississippi and its tributaries.

In 1702, Iberville invited the leaders of various Louisiana tribes to meet with him. When the invitation came, the Chickasaw were involved in a war with the Choctaw, but the tribes agreed to stop fighting long enough to attend Iberville's council. Seven Chickasaws journeyed down the Tombigbee to Mobile, where the Frenchman tried to court their allegiance by giving each delegate gifts, including beads, a knife, a hatchet, gunpowder, and a gun. Iberville urged the Chickasaw to end their war with the Choctaw, who had previously pledged loyalty to France. He warned the representatives from both tribes that if they did not end all their dealings with the British he would encourage neighboring tribes to attack them.

Despite Iberville's threat, the Chickasaw continued to trade with the British. The tribespeople loved the tools, fabrics, weapons, and other wares the British traders offered as well as the gifts the Englishmen had taken to distributing among them. A French trader occasionally turned up in Chickasaw territory, but usually his goods were of lower quality and his prices much higher than those the Chickasaw were accustomed to receiving from the English.

Largely owing to their attentiveness to the tribe's trade needs, the English were increasingly accepted by the Chickasaw. Jean-Baptiste Le Moyne, Sieur de Bienville—the brother of Iberville and the first governor of French Louisiana—came to see the tribe's support as unwinnable and to regard the Chickasaw as a threat to France's goal of control over the lower Mississippi Valley. The French began to hire Choctaw mercenaries to watch for Chickasaw raiding parties and to stalk English caravans bringing goods into Chickasaw territory. These actions drove the tribe even closer to the British.

There were other reasons that British influence among the Indians grew in the early decades of the 18th century. Some English traders married Chickasaw women, with whom they had children. These mixed-blood families felt a particularly strong bond to the British cause. Also during this period, the Chickasaw became increasingly dependent on European goods. As the Indians came to rely on these items, they gradually lost the knowledge of their traditional methods for making shelter, clothing, and other necessities. Reflecting this development, the center of

Chickasaw towns slowly shifted from the council house to traders' compounds where goods were displayed and exchanged.

The desire for English goods led Chickasaw men to kill more and more fur-bearing animals whose pelts they could trade. Because they began to exhaust the supply of animals in their own territory, they had to start hunting in lands far from home. Competition for hunting grounds increased among the many Indians throughout the region. Stronger tribes expanded their territory by waging war on smaller tribes, and the number of captives taken in battle grew. The Chickasaw had enslaved captives from other tribes long before Europeans arrived in their lands. But the value of slaves to English traders

This cross and monument near present-day Biloxi, Mississippi, mark the spot where the French explorer Pierre Le Moyne, Sieur d'Iberville first landed in North America in 1699. Iberville urged the Chickasaw to become allies of the French, but the tribe preferred dealing with the British.

A French map of the lower Mississippi Valley, drawn in about 1700. The homeland of the Chickasaw is designated with the label "Chicacha" to the right of the legend.

Mississippi, they devastated the small tribes living along the lower Arkansas and Red rivers. The ferocity of their slave raids led one Caddo chief to complain to French officials in 1717 that the Chickasaw had taken so many of his people prisoner that the few survivors had had to take refuge with other tribes. The officials countered by offering their Indian allies bounties for Chickasaw captives.

During this period, the British introduced the Chickasaw to several things that would change their way of life even more in the years to come. One was African slaves, whom English traders brought as servants into the Chickasaw Nation. The Chickasaw themselves, especially the mixed-bloods, soon bought black slaves to farm their fields. Through English influence, the Chickasaw also became horse owners. Mounted on these animals, the Chickasaw acquired still more horses by staging raids on tribes west of the Mississippi. The Chickasaw became singular horsemen and are credited with developing a special breed named after the tribe. Esteemed by Indians and white pioneers alike, the Chickasaw horse became famous throughout the Mississippi Valley for its long stride and endurance.

As the Chickasaw's loyalty to the British grew, so did their hostility toward the French. The tensions escalated into full-scale warfare in 1720, when the Chickasaw executed a French trader who was living in their territory. They believed the man had been spying

made the Chickasaw take more captives and even stage raids for the sole purpose of enslaving other Indians. They soon became the most notorious tribe involved in the slave traffic.

Initially, the Chickasaw raided only the Choctaw, Acolapissa, Chawasha, Yazoo, and other neighboring Indians for captives. But at the encouragement of British traders, they soon ranged into northern lands, falling on the hapless Cahokia and other groups. West of the on the Chickasaw and reporting back to Governor Bienville. Before this incident, the tribe had warred only on Indians allied to the French. But after the trader's execution, the angry Chickasaw began to strike French settlements and take Europeans captives. Chickasaw bands attacked French supply boats on the Mississippi as well and succeeded in closing the river to French shipping for four years. Bienville hired Choctaw mercenaries to battle the tribe's warriors. The governor seemed to take great satisfaction in that the French were fighting the first Chickasaw-French war "without shedding one drop of French blood."

The conflict, however, quickly began to take its toll on the French colonists. By 1723, commerce in Louisiana was at a standstill. French settlements to the north that depended on supplies from Louisiana were suffering, and French officials admitted that the war was "obliging our voyageurs to go and do their hunting on the upper part of the Wabash River, whereas in times of peace they would do it beyond the Arkansas." In 1724, the Council of War of Louisiana met to consider negotiating a peace with the Chickasaw. The council members decided that it was "to the advantage and welfare of the colony" to end the hostilities. Early in 1725, French officers led their Choctaw companies back to the Choctaw Nation. Once the invaders had retreated from Chickasaw territory, the tribe again allowed French boats to navigate the Mississippi and French hunters and traders

to roam the prairies and forests unmolested.

But the calm that had settled over the Mississippi Valley was deceptive. The Chickasaw and the British were in fact busy setting the stage for the second Chickasaw-French war. The first war had revealed to the British the strategic importance of the location of the Chickasaw Nation. The tribe's river raids, launched from the shore of their territory, had paralyzed shipping and communication on the Mississippi. The river was Louisiana's lifeline to the other French outposts in North America; without access to it, the British believed, the colony could easily be conquered. British officials came to see that with the help of their Chickasaw allies they could achieve their goal of wresting control of the Ohio and lower Mississippi valleys from the French.

Part of the British plan called for the Chickasaw to act as diplomats between them and French-allied tribes with whom the English wanted to trade. Some factions within these Indian groups were eager to turn against the French and pledge allegiance to the English in order to obtain low-priced British goods.

The Chickasaw's tactics were especially effective among the Natchez Indians. In November 1729, the Natchez attacked Fort Rosalie, a French settlement in their territory. The Indians killed at least 250 Frenchmen and took about 300 French women and children hostage. In retaliation, a force of French and Choctaw soldiers fell upon the

Natchez and almost succeeded in exterminating the entire tribe. Some of the few survivors fled to the Chickasaw Nation for refuge. The French insisted that the Chickasaw surrender the refugees, but the tribe refused. Perrier, Bienville's temporary successor as governor of Louisiana, then offered guns, ammunition, and bounties to warriors from several northern Indian tribes, such as the Iroquois and the Potawatomi, in exchange for assaulting towns in the Chickasaw Nation. The Chickasaw used two tactics to counter these raiding parties. They sent out their own warriors to attack the mercenaries' camps before the enemy could strike, and they offered presents to the paid Indian soldiers to shift their allegiance from the French to the Chickasaw and the British. Gifts of English goods also made friends of some factions among the Choctaw.

In 1732, when Bienville returned to his post as governor of Louisiana, he recognized that the French were quickly losing control of the region. In desperation, he became determined to annihilate the Chickasaw Nation and destroy the British advantage there. The governor first collected an army of more than 600 soldiers. He then ordered troops to construct a garrison named Fort Tombeckbe at the northern edge of the Choctaw Nation to serve as a base for his military campaign. Bienville sent couriers to Major Pierre d'Artaguette with a message to assemble French forces in Illinois country and bring them south to meet up with his army in the Chickasaw Nation, which he planned to attack at the end of March.

Bienville's forces were delayed waiting for provisions from France. After traveling up the Mobile River, his men finally arrived at Fort Tombeckbe on April 20. There the army was joined by a special corps of 600 Choctaws whose loyalty to the French was unquestioned.

In the meantime, d'Artaguette's army had met with disaster. They arrived in the Chickasaw Nation as planned and spent three weeks searching for Bienville and his soldiers. D'Artaguette was about to give up on the campaign when his scouts came upon a Chickasaw town called Chocolissa. Several soldiers urged the major to allow the army to plunder the town and make off with its stores of meat and grain. With the troops' provisions nearly exhausted, d'Artaguette agreed and led a charge against Chocolissa on the morning of March 25. From behind their palisade walls, the Chickasaw inhabitants surprised the troops with a hail of gunfire. A relief force of Chickasaw quickly arrived from a neighboring town. The Indian soldiers that made up much of d'Artaguette's force fled, and most of those fighters who stayed were killed. Major d'Artaguette himself was burned alive by the incensed Chickasaw.

The Chickasaw warriors then lay in wait for Bienville, whose approach they had learned of from papers taken from d'Artaguette and other captured officers. Ignorant of what had happened to d'Artaguette's army, Bienville arrived in Chickasaw country in late May. He and an aide named Chevalier de Noyan chose the town of Akia at the site of his force's initial attack. De Noyan selected 180 men and on the afternoon of May 26 led them in storming the town's fortifications. Soon, the French troops were caught in a deadly cross fire, which seriously wounded de Noyan and 52 others and killed 24 more. Bienville rushed in with reinforcements, but they were driven back. After three hours of brutal losses, the French commander ordered the invading force to retreat.

The French humiliation at the Battle of Akia only intensified France's determination to destroy the Chickasaw Nation. After three years of preparation, Bienville once again determined that his men were ready to redeem the ''honor of France.'' In an armada of riverboats, Bienville's 3,600-man army arrived in Chickasaw country in the early autumn of 1739. But before they could stage an attack, heavy and sustained rain set in. For three months, Bienville waited for the weather to improve. Finally, pressured by his officers, he sent Captain Pierre Celeron with 600 Canadian troops and Iroquois and Choctaw mercenaries on a 100-mile march toward the Chickasaw's settlements. The company's mission was to capture a Chick-

An engraving of Fort Rosalie, the French post that was attacked by Natchez Indians in 1729. Some of the few Natchez who survived the subsequent French retaliatory raids found refuge among the British-allied Chickasaw.

Sheffield's representation of the 1736 Battle of Akia, during which the Chickasaw soundly defeated the French troops led by Louisiana governor Jean-Baptiste Le Moyne, Sieur de Bienville. Warned in advance of French plans to attack the town of Akia, the inhabitants opened fire on the soldiers before they were able to storm the town's fortifications.

asaw town and then urge the Indians there to send a delegation to Bienville to negotiate a peace. Celeron's troops held one Chickasaw town for two days, but ultimately they were forced to retreat with losses.

Bienville's second failure to conquer the Chickasaw caused him to be removed from his post as governor. In 1743, when the Marquis de Vaudreuil, Bienville's successor, arrived in North America, he found the Chickasaw were still the most serious problem facing the French in Louisiana. The tribe continued to raid French settlements and attempt to persuade other Indians to renounce their loyalty to France. By

1752, Vaudreuil had had enough. He mustered an army of 700 regular French troops and a large number of Indian mercenaries and marched on the enemy nation, following the same route Bienville had taken in 1736. The Chickasaw wisely stayed inside their fortified towns. The French could not dislodge them and once again withdrew from the Chickasaw's territory without a victory.

The long struggle between France and England for control of North America continued until 1763, when Great Britain emerged victorious from a series of conflicts between the two powers, now known as the French and Indian

Wars. According to the Peace of Paris, which ended the fighting, England received all French claims in what is now Canada and the United States east of the Mississippi. France lost its lands west of the river to Spain, which in exchange for this huge tract gave up its colony in Florida to England.

Immediately following the French and Indian Wars, the British began to exert administrative control over the new lands it acquired through the Peace of Paris and over the Indians who lived there. In a document titled "Plan for the Future Management of Indian Affairs," the British government announced its intention "to place commercial and political relations with all of the Indians under a general system, administered by Crown officials." The plan divided the new British territory into two districts, designating the Ohio River as the boundary between them. Each district was to be governed by a superintendent assisted by a number of deputies. John Stuart was named superintendent of Indian affairs for the tribes south of the Ohio River, and John McIntosh was appointed as the deputy charged with dealing with the Chickasaw.

Being treated as subjects of a European king was new to the Chickasaw. Unlike the Choctaw, who had at least publicly appeared to accept French domination, the Chickasaw had always considered themselves a separate nation even as they pledged their loyalty to their British allies. Nevertheless, the Chickasaw accepted McIntosh and even relied on him for guidance in deal-

ing with his government in the years to come.

Although for the next decade the Chickasaw lived in relative peace, it was a turbulent period for the tribe. Several factors began to threaten their traditional social and political structure. One of the most alarming was a sizable influx in non-Indian settlers to their lands. In 1763, the British government had declared its lands west of the Appalachian Mountains and north of Florida off limits to settlers but had done little to punish non-Indians who ignored this decree. Portions of the Choctaw, Creek, and Cherokee nations were quickly overrun by settlers. Chickasaw territory, which was comparatively remote, escaped this invasion for a time. But soon immigrants from the coastal British colonies began to flock to Florida, which Britain divided into East and West Florida after taking control of the area from the Spanish. A favorite route to West Florida took these non-Indians through the heart of the Chickasaw homeland. Many never reached the British colony, choosing instead to settle illegally on Chickasaw territory.

At the same time, more British traders were coming to live among the Chickasaw. In 1763 alone, the number of traders increased from 30 to more than 100. Many did not have the licenses that the British government required of traders in Indian lands. Most also disregarded the government's prohibition on selling rum and other liquor. Chickasaw leaders repeatedly complained to McIntosh about the traders and about the corrupting influence that the rum they trafficked was having on the Chickasaw people.

The traditional Chickasaw leadership was also troubled by the growing power of the tribe's mixed-blood population. These children of British men and Chickasaw women had more experience with the language and manners of Europeans than most full-blood Chickasaw. As the number of non-Indians in Chickasaw territory grew, so did the importance of a leader's ability to communicate successfully with these outsiders. The mixed-bloods therefore had an advantage over the traditional full-blood chiefs in tribal politics and were subtly taking control over the management of the tribe. Among the most influential mixed-bloods were the five sons of James Logan Colbert, a Scotsman who came to live among the tribe in 1729 and married three Chickasaw women. The Colberts' major full-blood opponents, Payamataha and Piomingo, regularly voiced to Stuart and McIntosh their concerns about the ambitious mixed-bloods, who they felt were guided more by self-interest than by what was best for the tribe.

The Chickasaw's political infighting increased as the Spanish took administrative control over Louisiana, a process that was completed in 1769. Members of the old pro-French faction of Chickasaw sent a delegation to meet with Spanish officials. Still viewing the British as their enemy, this delegation sought protection from the Spanish as it had previously from the French.

Governor Bienville, whose inability to conquer the Chickasaw led to his dismissal in 1743.

Probably aware of this secret meeting, Superintendent Stuart and other British officials began to make a point of regularly reminding Chickasaw leaders of their pledge of loyalty to Great Britain.

The alliance with the Chickasaw proved crucial to the British during the American Revolution. Soon after the fighting broke out in 1775, British general Thomas Gage directed Stuart to rally the Chickasaw and other area Indians and "when the opportunity offers . . . to make them take arms against his Majesty's enemies."

Initially, most of the fighting was concentrated on the eastern seaboard, but by 1780 the Americans decided to launch a campaign in the southwestern portion of the territory claimed by the British. Seeing the Chickasaw Nation as a British stronghold in the area, Virginia governor Thomas Jefferson ordered that an American post be built in Chickasaw territory, at the mouth of the Ohio River. When the tribe discovered Fort Jefferson, an army of Chickasaw warriors led by James Colbert (a son of James Logan Colbert) marched on the post and initiated a siege that lasted almost a year. Cut off from supplies and suffering substantial losses, the American army finally retreated from the fort in June 1781.

The Chickasaw's successful resistance discouraged the American campaign in the British Southwest. The Spanish, who declared war on the British in 1779, began to pose a new threat to the tribe. After a Spanish army attacked West Florida, settlers from the British colony rushed into Chickasaw lands seeking refuge. These refugees joined the Chickasaw in attacks against nearby Spanish settlements. The Spanish forces did not have enough military strength to invade the Chickasaw Nation, but they did persuade the Kickapoo, a tribe of northern Indians who were allied to Spain, to stage raids on many Chickasaw towns. The Spanish also tried to undermine the Chickasaw's military campaign against them by courting the anti-British faction within the tribe.

The conflict finally ended in 1783 with victory for the Americans. According to the Treaty of Paris, which ended the war, the defeated British lost all their lands in North America. Their territory between the Appalachian Mountains and the Mississippi River, including the Chickasaw Nation, was granted to the newly formed United States, and East and West Florida were returned to Spain.

Having lost the support and protection of their European ally, the Chickasaw were thrown into a state of confusion. The gulf between their political factions grew deeper. Recognizing the Chickasaw's power and the strategic location of their territory, both Spain and the United States urged tribal members to sign treaties of alliance. Full-blood leader Piomingo and his followers advocated initiating diplomatic relations with the Americans, who seemed more like their old British friends. However, the anti-British faction, led by Wolf's Friend, still wanted to negotiate with the Spanish. Principal Chief Payamataha saw little difference between the two foreign powers and was attentive to the overtures of both.

The first Chickasaw treaty signed after the war was negotiated with the state of Virginia. At Piomingo's invitation, two Virginia officials met with a delegation headed by the Indian leader for two days in November 1783. The treaty that resulted provided for peace between Virginia and the Chickasaw Nation and defined the eastern boundary separating them.

The signing of the Treaty of Paris of 1783, in which England recognized the independence of the United States.

After hearing of the Chickasaw-Virginia treaty, the Spanish moved quickly to gain official support from Indians in the area. Early in 1784, Spain signed a treaty of alliance with the Creek. A key figure in the negotiations was Alexander McGillivray, a mixed-blood Creek leader who was extremely anti-American. At McGillivray's urging, a Chickasaw delegation agreed to meet with Spanish negotiators in June 1784. At this council, the delegation signed a treaty pledging the Chickasaw's loyalty to the king of Spain. The Spanish in turn agreed to protect the Chickasaw Nation from mutual enemies.

American officials had been too preoccupied with organizing their new national government to send representatives to meet with the Chickasaw and other southern Indians. But when word of the Chickasaw's treaty with Spain reached U.S. officials, they promptly appointed a commission of negotiators to invite tribal representatives of the Chickasaw, Cherokee, Choctaw, and Creek nations to a treaty council at Hopewell in what is now South Carolina. McGillivray urged the Chickasaw to honor their treaty with the Spanish, but members of Piomingo's faction journeyed to Hopewell, anyway. There they negotiated a treaty that declared the Chickasaw at peace with the Americans and "under the protection of the United States of America, and of no other sovereign whosoever." With the Treaty of Hopewell, the Chickasaw Nation's official relationship with a new and powerful ally began. ▲

An early-19th-century painting of Tishomingo, the last war chief of the Chickasaw.

LIVING
WITH
AMERICANS

By 1786, the Chickasaw Nation had pledged itself to two foreign governments—the United States and Spain. Each believed itself to be the tribe's only legitimate ally. The Chickasaw people themselves were split. Some had sought to make friends of the Americans. Others had welcomed the overtures of the Spanish. But still many others were in a state of confusion, unwilling to acknowledge allegiance to any outsiders and losing confidence in the ability of their own leaders to ensure the continued welfare of the tribe.

For a time, the contest between the United States and Spain for the Chickasaw's favor worked to the tribe's advantage. Both governments courted the Chickasaw with special treatment and with gifts of tobacco, blankets, rum, whiskey, knives, hatchets, and sometimes guns and gunpowder. At first, Spain seemed to be winning the ma-

jority of the Chickasaw to their side. The Spanish lavished attention on the tribe and especially on Chickasaw leaders who were already sympathetic to them. For instance, Wolf's Friend was paid $500 annually for promoting the Spanish cause among his tribespeople.

Probably the most influential pro-Spanish Indian leader during this period was Alexander McGillivray. McGillivray was determined to keep American settlers from moving westward into Indian land and believed that the best way to do so was to negotiate a solid alliance between Spain and all the large tribes in the Southeast. The Creek leader saw the pro-American faction of Chickasaw led by Piomingo as a potential threat to this plan. Aided by spies from the faction of Wolf's Friend, McGillivray kept a close eye on Piomingo. After discovering that the Chickasaw chief was meeting with a group of American traders, McGillivray sent a squad of Creek warriors into the Chickasaw Nation to attack the Americans. Under his direction, Creek war parties also began to ambush Indian traders on trails connecting Chickasaw lands and American settlements to the north. McGillivray tried as well to reduce Piomingo's power by setting the powerful Colbert family against him.

Piomingo reported to American officials McGillivray's attempts to undermine him. At first they ignored his request for aid. But after Piomingo and 50 Chickasaw troops joined American forces in a 1791 campaign against enemy Indians inhabiting American territory north of the Ohio River, the chief received more attention. By early 1792, the United States was sending large quantities of goods to the Chickasaw Nation to help convert pro-Spanish Indians into American supporters.

In August 1792, William Blount, governor of the territory south of the Ohio River, decided it was time to subvert McGillivray's efforts to build a Spanish-Indian alliance. He convened a council at Nashville, Tennessee, which was attended by delegations from the Chickasaw, Choctaw, Cherokee, and Creek tribes. Offering the leaders valuable goods "as proof of the sincere friendship of the United States," Blount stated that contrary to what Spanish officials had told them, the United States did not want and would not ask for their land. He added, "We wish you to enjoy your lands and be as happy as we ourselves are; nor do we want the

land of any red people; the United States have land enough."

After Blount's visit, the Creek stepped up their raids on travelers journeying through the Chickasaw Nation. Piomingo's faction decided to go to war with the Creek. The chief asked the U.S. government for aid and quickly received boatloads of supplies. With new weapons, the Chickasaw drove back the Creek warriors.

An even greater blow to the pro-Spanish faction occurred when McGillivray suddenly died in February 1793. Without his leadership, the Spanish-Indian alliance in the Southeast began to fall apart. Piomingo's followers took advantage of the situation and began raiding Creek settlements. By 1795, the Spanish-supported Creek were asking to negotiate a peace with the pro-American Chickasaw. After three years of councils, a lasting peace was established between the tribes.

The Spanish were rapidly losing influence among the Chickasaw, in part because of McGillivray's death but also because the United States had created a well-organized system for administering the Indians inhabiting its western frontier. The Americans' earlier inattention had allowed the Spanish to gain power in the Southeast; the new way of dealing with Indians, which called for constant contact between U.S. representatives and Indians, was designed to prevent this from happening again.

According to this plan, the War Department was charged with responsibility for all Indian affairs. Each tribe

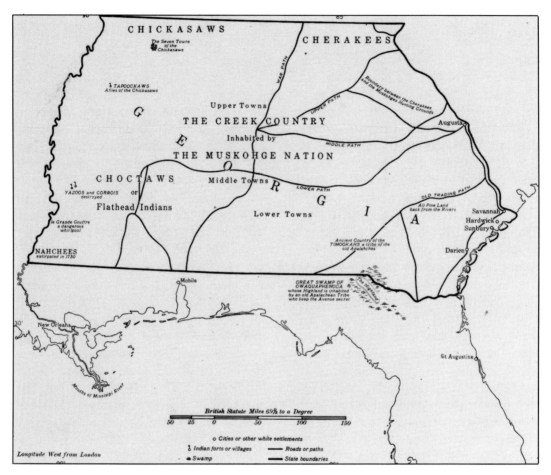

A simplified version of a 1788 British map of the state of Georgia, which at that time con-tained portions of present-day Alabama and Mississippi, including the Chickasaw homeland.

dealt with two officials—the governor of the territory in which they lived and an agent who usually resided among the tribe or in a nearby American set-tlement. The agent was to make sure the tribe remained loyal to the United States and was to enforce all federal laws applying to non-Indians and In-dians alike in the tribal territory. This official was also expected to help "civ-ilize" the Indians by teaching them about American society and encourag-ing them to give up hunting and take up agriculture in its place.

The first Chickasaw agent, James Robertson, was fairly successful. He had great respect for Piomingo, and his support of the full-blood leader helped to keep the more assertive mixed-bloods' bid for power in check, at least temporarily. In general, however, the Chickasaw were disappointed by their agents. In the 1790s and early 1800s, Chickasaw delegations often made the long journey to the nation's capital to speak directly with federal officials.

During this time, the United States also sought to manage Indian affairs by establishing control over trade with Indian groups. In 1796, Congress passed a law permitting the construction of publicly operated trading posts on Indian lands. The federal government built its first such post in the Chickasaw Nation at Chickasaw Bluffs six years later.

In the first two decades of the 19th century, the most important contact between the Chickasaw and the U.S. government was the negotiation of a series of four treaties. In spite of Superintendent Blount's earlier claims, the United States did wish to obtain title to Chickasaw lands in order to open them up to settlement by non-Indians. Federal commissioners were sent to the Chickasaw Nation in 1801, 1805, 1816, and 1818 to arrange the sale of portions of the tribe's territory to the government.

The commissioners soon discovered that the most effective way of getting what they wanted was to court the mixed-bloods, whose power had increased substantially. For instance, one commissioner reported that during the 1801 treaty negotiation, Chinubbee Minko, the principal chief, pointed to George Colbert and announced that the mixed-blood had been "fully empowered by the council" to discuss the

tribe's position with the American representatives. The Americans exploited the situation by providing the Colberts with goods and cash in exchange for their cooperation in negotiating treaties favorable to the government. The commissioners also used other devious methods—including getting Indian negotiators intoxicated and threatening tribespeople—to do their job.

In the Chickasaw's 1801 treaty, the tribe agreed to accept $700 in exchange for allowing the United States to make a wagon road through Chickasaw territory, following the course of the Natchez Trace, a path that, long used by traders, connected Nashville with the town of Natchez in what is now southwestern Mississippi. Five years later, another treaty granted the federal government all Chickasaw land to the north of the Tennessee River. For this cession, the tribe received $20,000, more than half of which went to pay the tribe's debt of $12,000 at the Chickasaw Bluffs trading post. This fulfilled a plan earlier proposed by President Thomas Jefferson:

> Establish among the Chickasaws a factory for furnishing them all the necessities and comforts they may wish (spirituous liquors excepted), encouraging them and especially their leading men, to run in debt for these beyond their individual means of paying; and whenever in that situation, they will always cede lands to rid themselves of debt.

The 1816 treaty resulted in the loss of the Chickasaw's title to all of their ter-

CHICKASAW LAND CESSIONS, 1805–32

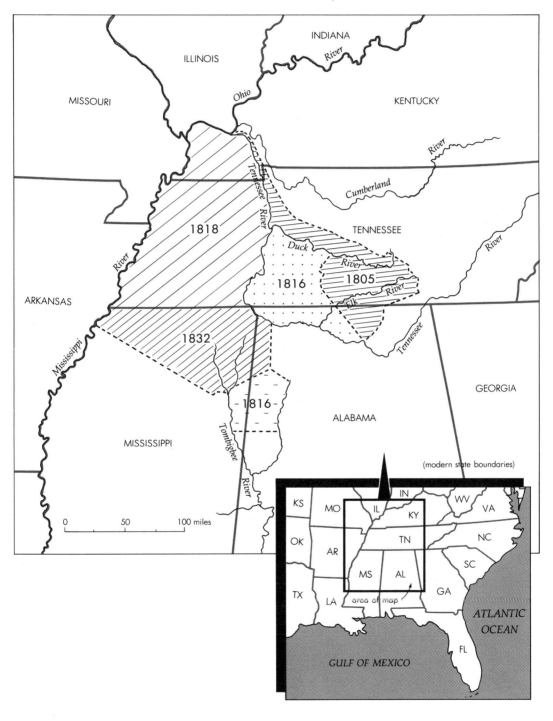

ritory stretching from the south side of the Tennessee River to the west bank of the Tombigbee, in exchange for a $12,000 annuity (annual payment) to be paid for 10 years. And in 1818, the tribe ceded all land north of the southern boundary of the state of Tennessee for a 15-year, $20,000 annuity. Through these treaties, the U.S. government in fewer than 20 years obtained nearly 20 million acres of the traditional Chickasaw homeland. All that remained of the once vast Chickasaw Nation was their land in what is now northeastern Mississippi and a small tract in present-day northwestern Alabama.

While the treaty commissioners were carving away portions of Chickasaw territory, another group of white Americans—Protestant missionaries— set about chipping away at the Chickasaw's traditional culture. The first missionary to live among the tribe was Presbyterian minister Joseph Bullen. Arriving in 1799, he resided in the Chickasaw Nation for four years. The Chickasaw were hospitable to Bullen during his stay, and he regularly preached to audiences of Indians, but he found few converts.

Nearly 20 years passed before a congressional act renewed missionary interest in the tribe. Passed in 1819, the Indian Civilization Act allocated $10,000 of federal money for Indian education. Missionaries were invited to request money from this fund for their work among tribes, with the stipulation that they teach Indians about academic subjects and agriculture as well as give them religious instruction.

Methodists, Baptists, and Presbyterians all visited the Chickasaw in the 1820s, but Presbyterian missionaries took the greatest advantage of the Indian education allocation. In 1820, representatives of the Cumberland Presbyterian Association founded a school named Charity Hall on the Tombigbee River. The institution stayed in operation until 1834. An even larger commitment to Chickasaw education was made by the South Carolina–Georgia Synod, a Presbyterian organization that sent two ministers, Rev. Thomas C. Stuart and Rev. David Humphries, to the Chickasaw Nation in 1820. Upon their arrival, they called on Levi Colbert. Through his influence, they obtained permission from the Chickasaw council to establish a mission. This six-building compound included a school named after President James Monroe. The Monroe school so impressed the Chickasaw that in 1824 the council set aside $5,000 in tribal funds for the construction of additional school buildings and $2,500 a year for their operation.

The Chickasaw school curriculum had three components. First, students were taught academic subjects, including geography, arithmetic, and reading and writing in English. Second, they were given vocational training. Boys learned about carpentry, farming, animal husbandry, and blacksmithing; girls were instructed in sewing, spin-

This engraved silver cross was made in Montreal, Canada, and brought to Mississippi in the 1830s by a Catholic missionary. In accordance with a common custom of the period, the missionary presented the cross to a Chickasaw chief as a token of friendship.

ning, weaving, and knitting. Third, the missionary teachers gave lessons in the Christian religion. The schools were closely monitored by the Chickasaw, and sometimes the principal chief paid visits to the institutions to check on the students' progress. The Chickasaw people's only criticism of the instructors was that they spent too much time preaching.

Missionaries were not the only non-Indians having an effect on the Chickasaw at this time. Many roads, including the Natchez Trace, were constructed through Chickasaw territory in the early 19th century, making it easier than ever for non-Indian settlers to come to their nation. In some respects, the contact the Indians had with these visitors proved beneficial to the tribe. The Chickasaw economy especially profited as the tribe developed a booming business in providing lodging and food for travelers. But the presence of the settlers also had ill effects. One of the most potentially damaging to the Chickasaw was that more and more non-Indians saw firsthand the lushness and fertility of the tribe's territory and began to covet the land for themselves.

Mississippi became a state in 1817, and Alabama followed suit in 1819. Soon leaders from both states began to press the federal government to open up Indian lands within their boundaries for white settlement. Legally, the U.S. government was bound by its treaties with the Chickasaw to protect the In-dians' lands from intruders, so the United States could comply with the states' requests only if a new agreement was reached with the tribe. To encourage the Chickasaw to consider negotiating more land cessions, the Mississippi and Alabama state legislatures passed a series of laws aimed at placing the Chickasaw Nation under their jurisdiction and reducing the power of Chickasaw leaders. Just as the states' officials had hoped, these laws sent the Chickasaw into a panic.

Even with this harassment, however, the tribe was not willing to cede more territory, as Secretary of War John C. Calhoun discovered during a visit from Levi Colbert in 1824. When Calhoun mentioned the idea, Colbert said that the Chickasaw would "sell no more land, despite pressure of the State of Mississippi." Considering the Colbert family's previous cooperation with U.S. officials, Calhoun was surprised by this response. But the secretary's proposal was very different from those made by earlier treaty commissioners. Most of land the tribe had ceded in the past consisted of hunting grounds. Losing this territory had certainly hurt the tribe, but it was in no way as devastating as it would be to cede their remaining land, the area where the Chickasaw's towns were located. To the Chickasaw, agreeing to any further land cessions was unthinkable.

In May 1826, the United States sent a delegation of three commissioners—William Clark, Thomas Hinds, and

John Coffee, one of three commissioners the federal government dispatched to the Chickasaw Nation in order to negotiate a treaty with the tribe in 1826.

John Coffee—to meet with Chickasaw and Choctaw representatives. Their mission was to persuade the two tribes to exchange their eastern homelands for territory located west of the Mississippi River. The idea of removing, or relocating, eastern tribes to western lands had a long history. The Louisiana Territory—the vast tract of land between the Mississippi and the Rocky Mountains—had passed from Spanish to French hands in 1800 and had then been purchased from France by President Thomas Jefferson in 1803. Jefferson had wanted Louisiana largely as an area to which he could remove tribes living east of the Mississippi when their homelands were desired by American settlers.

As the council opened, the commissioners tried to convince the Indians that it was to their advantage to agree to move west. The Americans explained:

> Your father the President proposes to give his Chickasaw children a fine tract of country on the other side of the Mississippi river, or *equal extent*, in exchange for their present lands. We know that you are attached to the country of your birth, and the lands in which the bones of your fathers are buried; but if the United States offers you one of equal or greater advantages, and are willing to pay you liberally for your improvements [houses, public buildings, and farms in the Chickasaw homeland], would not the nation best consult its real interest by making the exchange?

The Indian delegates were not impressed by this reasoning. Levi Colbert responded, "If we should exchange our lands for any other, . . . the consequences may be similar to transplanting an old tree, which would wither and die away, and we are fearful we would come to the same." The commissioners returned to Washington, D.C., without a treaty.

This failure only made the U.S. government more determined to negotiate the Chickasaw's removal. The next year, Thomas L. McKenney journeyed to the Chickasaw Nation to reopen talks. McKenney had been named commissioner of the newly created Bureau of Indian Affairs (BIA), the branch of the War Department charged with overseeing all dealings between Indians and the federal government. Unlike Clark, Hinds, and Coffee, the commissioner was concerned about the Indians' welfare. Without threats, he tried to persuade Levi Colbert and other leaders to reconsider:

> Brothers—Whilst then you cherish a sacred remembrance for the bones of your Fathers, forget not to provide for your children, and never stop a moment, but hasten with all speed to place them in a situation that will secure them against the evils that your Fathers endured. . . . This Brothers, is Wisdom.

The Chickasaw again refused to negotiate, but they did agree at least to send a scouting party to inspect the area in which the United States wanted to relocate them.

U.S. officials were pleased with this news but became anxious as the Chickasaw took their time in putting together their exploratory party. Only after being pressured by agents and after receiving an allocation of $15,000 from Congress to finance the expedition did the tribe assemble a party of 12 leaders to make the journey. Led by Levi Colbert, the expedition toured portions of what is now Oklahoma in the winter of 1828. When the expedition returned home, its members reported to the council, which then informed officials in the U.S. government that the Chickasaw were disappointed in the western lands and would not "consent to remove to a country destitute of a single corresponding feature of the one in which we presently reside."

The Chickasaw had once again succeeded in putting off efforts to move them west, but their relief was short-lived. Two events occurring in 1830 would finally break the tribe's resolve to remain in its homeland. One was the passage by Congress of the Indian Removal Act, which authorized the president to negotiate directly with eastern tribes for their removal. The act had little practical effect on the way the United States conducted its removal program, but by expressing the federal government's determination to obtain the tribe's eastern lands, it made removal seem inevitable to the Chickasaw. Also in 1830, the state of Mississippi passed statutes that abolished the Chickasaw tribal government and tribal laws. Chickasaw leaders were subject to a $1,000 fine and imprisonment if they attempted to govern their people. The tribe immediately asked President Andrew Jackson to stop Mississippi from enforcing these laws, which violated the Chickasaw's treaties with the U.S. government. Jackson, a longtime supporter of the removal policy, refused to help.

Suddenly, the Chickasaw found themselves with no legal protection from the non-Indian settlers willing to use any means possible to take control of the tribe's lands. Now they had two choices: to watch squatters invade and overtake their territory, leaving the Chickasaw with nothing, or to cede their land to the government and receive title to a tract in the West. The Chickasaw leaders chose what seemed their only true option. Soon U.S. officials received word that the Chickasaw were willing to negotiate. ▲

The interior of the Pontotoc Creek council house during the negotiation of the Chickasaw's 1830 removal treaty. Tribal leaders later implored U.S. officials to nullify the Pontotoc agreement, which the Indians claimed they had signed under duress.

THE

TRAIL
OF TEARS

The process of dissolving the Chickasaw Nation in the East began in August 1830, when a Chickasaw delegation from Mississippi arrived in Franklin, Tennessee, to negotiate a removal treaty with the U.S. government. In addition to Commissioners John A. Eaton and John Coffee, the United States was represented by President Andrew Jackson. His presence signaled to Americans the importance of the council. But the Chickasaw needed no foreign dignitary to explain to them the significance of the event. They knew that the outcome of the council would determine their fate and possibly even dictate whether or not they could survive as a people.

Pressured by the federal and state governments to leave their territory, the Chickasaw leaders were not in a strong negotiating position. Nevertheless, they drove a hard bargain with the commissioners. They shrewdly asked for as much compensation as possible for their homeland and the improvements they had made to it. Eaton and Coffee struck down many of the Chickasaw's demands and urged their negotiators to "make their propositions reasonable, but not exorbitant." Both sides compromised, and in the end the Chickasaw had negotiated a relatively generous settlement.

As signed, the Franklin treaty provided for the cession of all remaining Chickasaw lands in exchange for a tract west of the Mississippi. The United States was to pay for the tribe's traveling costs, provide the Chickasaw with food for 1 year after their emigration, and give them a $15,000 annuity for 20 years. The Chickasaw were to send a delegation to the West to choose their new territory, but the treaty added that

if, after proper examination, a country suitable to their wants and conditions can not be found; then, it is stipulated and agreed, that this treaty, and all its provisions, shall be considered null and void.

Political and business leaders in Mississippi were ecstatic when they heard that the Chickasaw had finally ceded their homeland. At a celebration in Natchez, they toasted President Jackson for his role in coercing the tribe into negotiating with the government: "He found one half of our territory occupied by a few wandering Indians. He will leave it in the cultivation of thousands of grateful freemen."

But the Chickasaw were not to disappear from Mississippi so quickly. In October 1830, a Chickasaw expedition set out for the West and once again returned with the opinion that no land there was suitable for the tribe. Levi Colbert sent a letter to this effect to President Jackson. Because of the clause in the Franklin treaty granting the Chickasaw the right to reject unsuitable territory, this letter nullified the agreement.

The Chickasaw, however, were soon willing to negotiate again because living in Mississippi was rapidly growing more difficult. With tribal law abolished, many non-Indians felt there was

nothing to stop them from intruding on tribal land. Settlers flooded into the Chickasaw Nation. Now subject to state laws, some Indians were imprisoned or fined on trumped-up charges by vindictive whites.

Commissioner Coffee was sent to reopen talks with the Chickasaw. This time, sensing the Chickasaw's vulnerable position, Coffee pressured the tribal delegation by threatening to withhold the Chickasaw's annuities if the representatives did not agree to his terms. The commissioner also had an advantage because Levi Colbert, the Chickasaw's major opponent of removal, was seriously ill and could not speak on behalf of the tribe at the council.

On October 20, the Chickasaw signed a new removal treaty at their council house on Pontotoc Creek. The Pontotoc treaty stated that the tribe's eastern lands were to be surveyed immediately. Each Chickasaw adult would be assigned a specific tract, or allotment, on which he or she would live before emigrating west. The size of a person's allotment depended on several factors, including the size of the family and the number of slaves owned. When vacated, all the allotments and any surplus Chickasaw land not assigned would be sold by the federal government, and the proceeds would be placed in a general Chickasaw tribal fund. From this fund, the Chickasaw were eventually to reimburse the government for the cost of the survey, the land sales, and the tribe's removal.

President Andrew Jackson, an unswerving advocate of removal, met with a Chickasaw delega-tion in 1830 in Franklin, Tennessee. When the leaders reluctantly agreed to leave their home-land, Mississippi state officials toasted Jackson, saying, "He found one half of our territory occupied by a few wandering Indians. He will leave it in the cultivation of thousands of grate-ful freemen."

A portion of the signature page of the Pontotoc treaty, which many Chickasaw leaders, including Tishomingo, George Colbert, and Levi Colbert, signed by marking the document with an X.

In the months to come, Chickasaw delegations made a series of trips to Washington, D.C., to denounce the Pontotoc treaty and Coffee's methods of compelling the Indians to sign it. After much debate, federal officials finally agreed to amend the treaty in May 1834. In the amended treaty, individual allotments were enlarged, and the proceeds of their sale were to be given directly to the allotments' owners as long as they were deemed competent to handle their own business affairs by a special group of tribal leaders named as the Chickasaw Commission. The money due to tribespeople judged incompetent would be placed in the tribal fund until the Chickasaw were in their western lands.

In preparation for carrying out the amended treaty's terms, the federal government made a list of all the people of the Chickasaw Nation. Included in this roll were 6,070 individuals—4,914 Chickasaws and 1,156 slaves. Only one-third of the Chickasaw Nation's 6,422,400 acres was assigned as allotments. The more than 4 million acres of surplus land were sold over an 18-year period through public auctions, the first of which was held in January 1836. These auctions and the selling of the individual allotments attracted swarms of land speculators, many eager to cheat the Indians out of their land. Some Chickasaw fell victim to their schemes, but other Indians negotiated good prices for their allotments and used the money to buy livestock, tools, and other goods they would need in their western home.

Between 1834 and 1837, the Chickasaw repeatedly sent parties to the West to find an area in which to locate their new tribal nation. As more and more whites settled in their homeland, the pressure on these explorers grew. Finally, in January 1837, tribal leaders decided to accept an invitation from the Choctaw to occupy a portion of the land given them in their removal treaty. In the Treaty of Doaksville, the Chickasaw agreed to pay the Choctaw $530,000 for the right to live in the western two-thirds of the new Choctaw Nation. The Choctaw's western home was an enormous tract between the Canadian and Red rivers, in the southern portion of the region the government had designated as Indian Territory (now Oklahoma). The Choctaw had been removed there between 1830 and 1832 but had only settled the easternmost area of this large region. According to the Doaksville treaty, the Chickasaw would become citizens of the Choctaw Nation, and both Chickasaw and Choctaw individuals were permitted to settle anywhere within the Choctaw Nation's boundaries.

The government began to make plans for the Chickasaw's removal almost immediately. The secretary of war appointed A. M. M. Upshaw to organize the preparations and supervise the journey. Upshaw met with Chickasaw leaders, assembled the first removal party, and appointed John M. Millard

to lead it west. In late June, about 450 Chickasaws, with a train of wagons crammed with their possessions, set out toward Indian Territory.

On July 4, the removal party crossed the Mississippi River. A few days later heavy rains set in, making travel difficult. Marching in rain-soaked clothes, many people came down with dysentery. Even after the rain stopped, the emigrants were only able to travel about 13 miles a day.

When the party reached Little Rock, Arkansas, most of the Chickasaw decided to defy Millard by traveling southwest toward Choctaw settlements on the Red River instead of continuing north along the Arkansas River, the route the American guide recommended. With only 170 party members, Millard continued on the northern route and reached the Choctaw Nation in early August. Millard then rushed to join the rest of the Chickasaw, whom he found sick and straggling on at a slow pace. Many died as they continued their march; burying the dead took so much time that they covered even fewer miles in a day than before. Millard grew impatient with the pace and threatened to request the government to send troops who would compel the Chickasaw to move faster "at the point of a bayonet." The defeated Indian emigrants agreed to hurry, and on September 5, the group finally arrived in the settlements near Fort Towson, in the southeastern corner of the Choctaw Nation. Upshaw's relief at finally reaching

APPROXIMATE REMOVAL ROUTES OF THE CHICKASAW

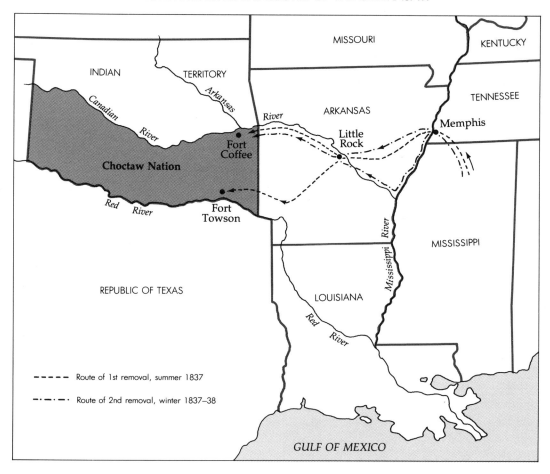

Indian Territory quickly turned to anxiety when the commissioner of Indian affairs reprimanded him for allowing most of the Chickasaw in his care to deviate from the removal route the government had originally charted. The commissioner authorized Upshaw in the future to withhold food rations from Chickasaw emigrants who refused to cooperate.

By the fall of 1837, federal officials had gathered nearly 4,000 of the Chick-asaw still in Mississippi and Alabama in emigration camps, in preparation for their removal. Upshaw decided to transport the next removal party up the Mississippi by steamers that would be boarded at Memphis. En route to the city, the Chickasaw learned that hundreds of Creek Indians, who were also being removed to Indian Territory, had been killed when the boiler in the steamer carrying them upriver exploded. Terrified by this news, nearly

1,000 Chickasaws refused to board the steamers and told Upshaw that they would travel by land instead. Upshaw threatened to stop giving this group rations, just as the commissioner of Indian affairs had told him to do. But when Konope, the spokesman for the land party, reminded him that the Chickasaw themselves were paying for their traveling expenses, Upshaw backed down and allowed them to follow their own route west. The 3,000 Chickasaws traveling by river reached Fort Coffee in the Choctaw Nation in about 10 days; the 1,000-person land party arrived there about 4 weeks later.

By early 1838, most Chickasaw Indians were in Indian Territory. Upshaw declared that the tribe's removal was complete, and the next year he dismissed his staff. But Upshaw's actions were premature. At least 500 Chickasaws were still living in the Southeast. Throughout the 1840s, small parties of Chickasaw made the long, arduous journey to their new home without the benefit of the government's promised assistance.

Although the Chickasaw suffered greatly, their removal to Indian Territory along the Trail of Tears, as their removal route later became popularly known, was not as terrible as the experience was for the Cherokee or the Creek. The Chickasaw, however, met with immense difficulties upon arriving in their western lands.

Disease was a persistent problem for the Chickasaw in the late 1830s and early 1840s. Living in crowded emigrant camps among the Choctaw, most suffered from dysentery or, even worse, smallpox. A smallpox epidemic in 1838 killed more than 500 Chickasaws and Choctaws.

Those who survived were faced with hunger and malnutrition, owing to the mismanagement of the Chickasaw removal by the U.S. government. According to the terms of the Pontotoc treaty, the United States was to provide food to the Chickasaw for one year after their move to the West. This provision was intended to ensure the Indians' survival during the period before they could plant and harvest their first crop in their new homeland. Unlike many removed southeastern tribes, the Chickasaw were expected to reimburse the government for their rations from their tribal fund.

When the Chickasaw removal was still in the early planning stages, federal officials began to purchase flour, pork, and corn without thought to the schedule of the removal parties. Long before the Chickasaw emigrants even arrived in Indian Territory, thousands of barrels of food bought for them had spoiled, and the cost of the rotten provisions was charged to the Chickasaw's account.

Needing a new system of providing rations for the emigrating Indians, the government decided to contract with private companies for the purchase and distribution of food to the tribe. This plan proved disastrous for the Chickasaw. Most of the contractors were dishonest. Knowing that the Indians, not

The official seal of the Chickasaw Nation, which has been affixed to legal documents of the tribe since 1867. The warrior depicted on the shield is Tishomingo, one of the hundreds of Chickasaws who died on the tribe's brutal Trail of Tears.

the United States, were ultimately paying for the rations, they believed that they could charge high prices for inadequate food and have their crime go unnoticed or, at the very least, unpunished. After their journey to the West, the Chickasaw were greeted with rations of such poor quality as to be barely edible. Some pork they were given was so rancid that even the starving would not eat the meat for fear it would kill them. In order to survive, the Chickasaw had to purchase food at inflated prices from Indian settlers who were already established in the area.

For years, Chickasaw leaders complained bitterly to federal officials about the contractors and their spoiled rations. In December 1841, Secretary of War J. C. Spencer finally took action. He sent Major Ethan Allen Hitchcock to Indian Territory to investigate the situation. Hitchcock was shocked by what he discovered. He found that the Chickasaw had been billed for $200,000 worth of spoiled food and charged more than $700,000 for rations they had never even obtained.

Hitchcock submitted a detailed report of the abuses of the contractors to Spencer, who promptly labeled the report as confidential. Even after members of Congress requested to see Hitchcock's findings, Spencer refused to make them public. When Congress persisted, the secretary claimed that the report had been lost in the War Department's files.

Eleven years later, Congress decided to launch its own investigation. It confirmed Hitchcock's allegations against the ration contractors and also uncovered evidence that led to charges of fraud against some companies whose services had been purchased during the Chickasaw removal. For instance, the captain of the steamers that took 3,000 Chickasaws up the Mississippi counted the 1,000 emigrants who opted to take a land route as passengers as well. The tribe was charged $37,749 in passage fees for people who had never even boarded the captain's boats. Still another 35 years passed before this scandal was resolved. In 1887, almost 50 years after Hitchcock originally filed his report, the Chickasaw tribe won its court case, *The Chickasaw Nation v. the United States*, and was awarded $240,164. Although a victory for the Chickasaw people, this small measure of justice, so late in coming, could do nothing to relieve the suffering inflicted by the tribe's Trail of Tears. ▲

A Chickasaw boy, photographed in the mid-19th century.

BRAVING
THE
WEST

The Chickasaw's early years in the West were not easy. The trauma of being uprooted from their homeland was felt by every tribal member but was especially serious for the full-blood Chickasaw. They and their ancestors had bemoaned the loss of more and more Chickasaw traditions in the centuries since the tribe first had contact with non-Indians. But in the decades immediately following removal, the full-bloods were forced to witness the disintegration of most of the few tribal values that still existed.

One of the greatest losses was their traditional form of government. When the Chickasaw first arrived in Indian Territory, they settled in the eastern Choctaw Nation in 5 emigrant camps situated about 100 miles from one another. The camps were intended to be temporary, but exhausted from their removal, the Chickasaw were not eager to leave these settlements to travel farther west to their own territory. Living in these camps made it impossible for the Chickasaw to reestablish the government they had had in the East. In Mississippi and Alabama, they had lived in many towns, each of which sent a representative to the national council. But in the West, where they had only five settlements, the structure of the national council had to be changed. However, the Chickasaw leadership was in such a state of confusion after removal and the death of Levi Colbert in 1834 that no one faction was able to get enough power to dictate how the Chickasaw would now govern themselves.

Compounding this problem were the provisions of the 1837 Doaksville treaty, which the Chickasaw had negotiated with the Choctaw. According to the agreement, the Chickasaw were citizens of the Choctaw Nation and subject to its laws. In 1838, the Choctaw drafted a constitution that divided their nation into four districts—three from Choctaw territory, one from the lands to be inhabited by the Chickasaw. Each district was to send 10 people to a 40-member national council. From the outset, the Chickasaw were unhappy with the plan. The Chickasaw council members would be outnumbered by Choctaw representatives by three to one; therefore, the Chickasaw feared that they would have little voice in the government of the Choctaw Nation.

The Choctaw also grew uncomfortable with the arrangements made in the Treaty of Doaksville. When they invited the Chickasaw to share their territory, they expected the Chickasaw immigrants to want to live in the lands the treaty designated for them, to the west of the Choctaw settlements. The Choctaw became irritated when the Chickasaw showed little interest in leaving the immigrant camps. One reason the Chickasaw stayed was their supposedly huge tribal fund. Before the federal government's frittering away of this money during the removal process was uncovered, the tribe believed its fund included $3 million. The yearly interest made on this money was to be distributed among the tribespeople annually. Assuming that each individual's payment would be about $14 to $18—more than enough for a person to live comfortably for an entire year in the mid-19th century—the Chickasaw did not

have much incentive to move westward and establish their own farms and businesses. Major Hitchcock noted other consequences of the Chickasaw's expectation of interest income:

> Their reliance upon their trust fund for money has induced a general neglect of industry and has resulted in a dependence upon external resources. This has thrown the . . . greater portion of the tribe, into the hands of creditors who on their part having looked to the prospective wealth of the tribe, have willingly brought them into debt.

Another reason, given by the Chickasaw, for the tribe's refusal to move into their district was their fear of attack by other Indians who already occupied this land. Several tribes, such as the Kickapoo and Shawnee, had established settlements in the area. Other western groups, including the Kiowa and Comanche, regularly hunted in the region.

Eager for the Chickasaw to leave their districts, the Choctaw pressured Chickasaw leaders to ask the U.S. government for a promise of military protection against these western Indians. In 1841, the secretary of war responded by ordering that a military post, to be named Fort Washita, be constructed in the southeastern portion of the Chickasaw District. But even with U.S. soldiers stationed in their new territory to protect them, Chickasaw settlers were slow to move west. In 1844, three-

This photograph of Annie Guy, a girl of Chickasaw and white ancestry, shows the influence non-Indian dress and customs had on many of the Chickasaw after their removal to Indian Territory.

fourths of the tribal population still lived among the Choctaw. Chickasaw migration increased in the early 1850s, especially after the United States built a second garrison, Fort Arbuckle, in their lands. By 1853, 90 percent of the Chickasaw lived in the Chickasaw District.

In their new territory, the Chickasaw became more industrious. Instead of living in towns as they had in their southern homeland, the tribespeople set up isolated farms as most rural non-Indians did. The Chickasaw's principal settlements—Pontotoc, Fort Washita, Colbert, Fort Arbuckle, Tishomingo City, and Burney—functioned primarily as centers of trade for people residing in the general area.

In the 1850s, the mixed-bloods established a variety of businesses. Some operated lumber mills or cotton gins. Others became traveling merchants who journeyed north into the Great Plains to deal with Indian groups there. A few Chickasaw established spas at oil springs on the southern edge of the Arbuckle Mountains. Advertising in Arkansas, Texas, and Louisiana newspapers, these spa operators built thriving businesses by promoting oil baths as remedies for all types of chronic diseases.

But still the Chickasaw's most important economic activity was agriculture. In their new territory, the tribe had more fertile land than they could farm. Especially rich was the soil along river bottoms. Chickasaw farmers flocked to these areas. Full-blood fam-

ilies tended to cultivate small fields of about 3 to 10 acres. Occasionally they would have surplus grain, but usually they themselves ate everything they harvested. In contrast, many mixed-bloods operated commercial farms on which most of the labor was performed by black slaves. Their plantations ranged in size from 100 to more than 1,000 acres.

The Chickasaw found that their district was also ideal for raising livestock. The grassy prairie provided plenty of grazing land capable of sustaining large herds of animals year-round. Continuing to breed horses as they had in the East, the Chickasaw also began to raise cattle, sheep, goats, and hogs.

As the tribe adjusted to its new environment, a new Chickasaw society emerged that combined their past and present. For instance, the Chickasaw still enjoyed attending annual gatherings, but the purpose of the meetings had changed. In the East, people came together once a year for the traditional Busk Festival; in the West, they met annually at Fort Washita to collect annuities from federal officials. Before the annuity distributions began, the gathered Chickasaw visited with one another and played the same games that had amused their ancestors. But the entertainment at the fort also included drinking parties, in which some Chickasaw consumed huge quantities of whiskey sold to them by Texas bootleggers. The tribe's adoption of this non-Indian vice worried tribal leaders and led them to form temperance societies

(continued on page 73)

A CULTURE ON EXHIBIT

During the Chickasaw's nearly 450 years of contact with non-Indians, the tribe has been compelled to abandon many of its traditional customs and beliefs. The Museum of Chickasaw Indian Culture in Ada, Oklahoma, is now attempting to reverse this situation. Through the museum, the people of the contemporary Chickasaw Nation are preserving what many of their white neighbors in the past had sought to destroy.

The museum, which is open to both tribal members and visitors to the Chickasaw Nation, exhibits many different types of artifacts that convey the richness of Chickasaw culture. Some are tools that the Chickasaw created and used for centuries to farm or hunt their food or to make their shelter and clothing from the resources of their environment. Others are ceremonial ornaments that played a central role in their ancient religious rituals.

The museum's collection also illustrates the Chickasaw's divided history by exhibiting objects from both their ancestral southeastern homeland and the new nation they forged in what is now Oklahoma. By viewing these testaments to the past, the Chickasaw continually renew their pride in the present.

A replica of the sacred pole that led the ancestors of the Chickasaw to their homeland. According to legend, the Chickasaw's forebears placed a staff into the ground each night during their migration from the west. Then, each morning, they set out in the direction the pole was leaning.

A reproduction of the type of beaded crown traditionally worn by Chickasaw leaders during ceremonies.

A medicine bag made from tanned leather and decorated with beads and pieces of metal. In the 18th and 19th centuries, herb remedies were carried in bags such as this.

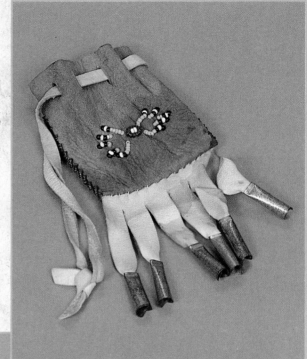

This type of leather bag is sometimes worn today by Chickasaw women during tribal get-togethers known as powwows.

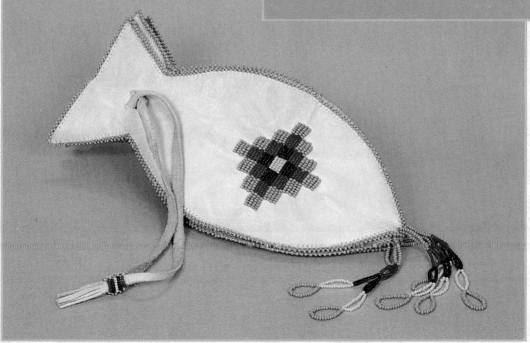

A hawk-feather fan with a tanned-leather handle. Such fans were first made by the Chickasaw in the 16th century and are still used today by tribal members during powwows.

A rattle made from a turtle shell and adorned with feathers. Turtle-shell rattles were traditionally played during ceremonial dances.

A pair of medicine horns. Traditional healers cured some patients by making an incision in an afflicted body part, placing the wide end of a medicine horn over the cut, and sucking the horn's tip to remove the "bad blood" from the wound.

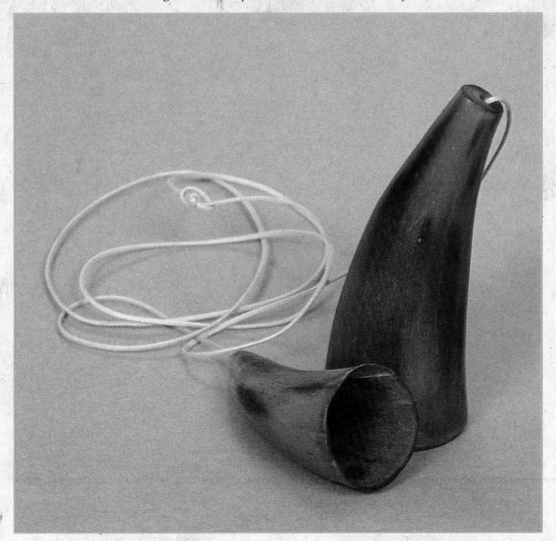

A wooden pestle for grinding corn. Many of the Chickasaw's traditional foods were made from pulverized corn.

A stone and metate, which the tribe used to grind corn, nuts, and berries.

This baked-clay pot was excavated from the Chickasaw's traditional homeland. It was used for holding drinking water.

A blow gun and two darts tufted with dandelion flowers. When the Chickasaw lived in what is now Mississippi, they used this type of weapon to hunt game, including deer and rabbits.

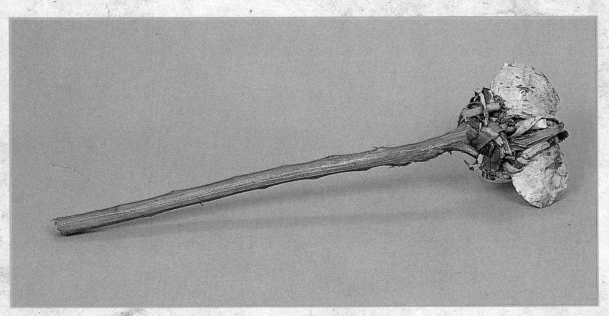

From the 15th to the 18th century, the Chickasaw cut wood with stone-headed hatchets such as this.

(continued from page 64)

to discourage drinking among the Chickasaw.

By the 1850s, many Chickasaw, especially the mixed-bloods, wore the same type of clothing, lived in the same type of log houses, and ate the same type of food as did non-Indians in the West. Although many 19th-century whites considered education the best way to "civilize" Indians, the Chickasaw made these changes without the influence of schooling. During the 15 years following their removal, the Chickasaw had no schools of their own. A few children attended Choctaw schools, and some students were sent to the Choctaw Academy, a boarding school in Kentucky. But the vast majority of the Chickasaw people received no formal education during this period.

As it had in the East, the influence of missionaries finally moved the Chickasaw to develop a school system. In the 1840s and 1850s, Baptists, Roman Catholics, Methodists, and Presbyterians came to preach Christianity to the

The first Chickasaw council house in Indian Territory, which was built in 1848 in the town of Tishomingo.

Bloomfield Academy, a school for Chickasaw girls, opened in 1852 as part of the tribe's efforts to reestablish their school system in the West.

Chickasaw, but the Methodists pressured the tribe most to establish schools. In late 1844, Methodist officials negotiated with tribal leaders to create a system of local upper and lower schools. Most of the financing was to come from the Chickasaw tribal fund. The teachers and laborers to build the schools were to be provided by the Methodists.

The Chickasaw Manual Labor Academy, opened in 1851, was the first school in the Chickasaw District. Between 1854 and 1857, four more upper schools were built. During the same period, a system of elementary schools was also established.

In the 1850s, the Chickasaw also turned their attention to resolving their problems with being part of the Choctaw Nation. As they became increasingly settled, their irritation with their minority status within the Choctaw Nation grew. Believing they could hold little sway in the Choctaw council, the Chickasaw had almost no enthusiasm for participating in the national government. The tribespeople had been living in the West several years before they even bothered to elect the full 10 representatives they were allowed to have in the national council.

Chickasaw leaders became convinced that the Chickasaw District needed its independence from the Choctaw Nation. The Chickasaw demanded their own national government, claiming that they owned the Chickasaw District, even though the Treaty of Doaksville stated that they had only purchased the right to settle there from the Choctaw. They took this and other complaints against the Choctaw to federal officials, often overstating their persecution to gain U.S. support for their campaign to separate themselves from the Choctaw Nation. In an 1851 letter to the commissioner of Indian affairs, Chickasaw leader Winchester Colbert claimed that his people were "completely at the mercy of the Choctaws, and every Chickasaw feels that he is oppressed by them."

In 1855, Chickasaw and Choctaw commissioners finally met with U.S. officials in Washington, D.C., to resolve the tribes' many disagreements. They negotiated an agreement that essentially dissolved the Treaty of Doaksville.

The Chickasaw were to have their own nation, made up of the eastern half of the old Chickasaw District. In exchange for $150,000, the Choctaw were to grant the Chickasaw full title to this land. The western half of the district was to be shared by the two tribes. Needing land to provide a western home for several recently removed Indian groups, the United States agreed to lease this region for $800,000. The lease payment was to be divided between the tribes, with the Choctaw receiving $600,000 and the Chickasaw getting $200,000. Citizens of the Chickasaw Nation were also to have citizenship in the Choctaw Nation and vice versa.

Even before the Treaty of 1855 was ratified by Congress, the Chickasaw held a constitutional convention to set down guidelines for the government of the Chickasaw Nation. The Chickasaw constitution, drafted in 1856, called for the election every two years of a "chief magistrate," who would be referred to as "governor." Like the U.S. government, the Chickasaw's national government would have a supreme court and a council consisting of a house of representatives and a senate. The constitution also defined four counties—Pontotoc, Pickens, Tishomingo, and Panola—within the Chickasaw Nation.

In the fall of 1856, the election for the first governor of the Chickasaw Nation was held. During the voting, the candidates stood in a field outside the national council house. According to the constitution, only free males, 19

THE CHICKASAW NATION AND VICINITY, 1855

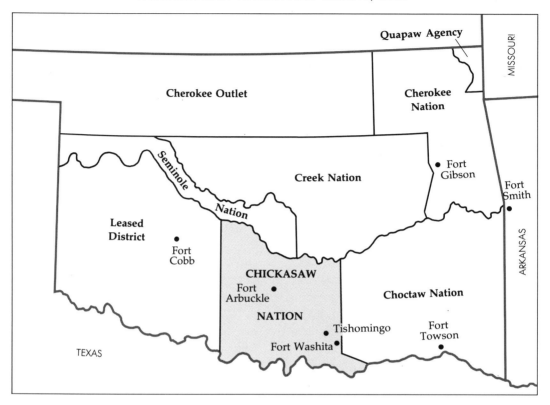

years or older, were eligible to participate in the election. To cast their vote, the Chickasaw men lined up behind the candidate of their choice. When the people in all the lines were counted, candidate Cyrus Harris was declared the winner.

In only a few decades, the Chickasaw had made a new life for themselves in the West. Unable to rebuild their old society, they had developed a hybrid way of life, combining their traditions with new customs they created themselves or borrowed from others. But this society, too, became threatened in the early 1860s by conflicts not of the Chickasaw's making. In the spring of 1861, the American Civil War began as 11 Southern states seceded from the United States to form their own nation, the Confederate States of America. Indian Territory was soon in turmoil, as tribes realized that they would quickly have to decide whether to support the Union or the Confederacy.

The question of allegiance became even more pressing for the Chickasaw in April 1861, when Confederate troops from Texas entered Indian Territory from the south. Outnumbered, the U.S.

troops at Fort Arbuckle and Fort Washita in the Chickasaw Nation, Fort Cobb in the Leased District, and Fort Smith just north of the Choctaw Nation evacuated their posts to evade capture by the rebels. Despite the United States's treaty promise to protect Chickasaw territory from foreign troops, the federal government had left the Chickasaw to fend for themselves against the enemy soldiers occupying their land.

Officials in the Confederate government recognized that the United States's action might help move the Chickasaw to pledge allegiance to their side. They also suspected that the Chickasaw and other Indian Territory tribes might be naturally sympathetic to the Southern cause. After all, many of the influential leaders of these groups were slaveholders, and after suffering so many abuses from the U.S. government during and after removal, their loyalty to the United States was probably not heartfelt. In hopes of gaining the Indians' support and possibly their military help, the Confederacy appointed Commissioner Albert Pike to try to negotiate treaties of alliance with the Chickasaw, Choctaw, Creek, Seminole, and Cherokee, who were commonly known as the Five Civilized Tribes because of their adoption of many non-Indian customs.

At a council at North Fork Town in the Creek Nation, Pike found that the Confederate officials' hunch was largely correct. The commissioner negotiated a treaty with the Creek, another with the Chickasaw and the Choctaw, and a third with the Seminole. Only the Cherokee chose not to commit themselves to the Confederate cause.

In the Chickasaw and Choctaw's treaty with the South, the tribes acknowledged that they were now under the protection of the Confederate States of America and "of no other power or sovereign whatever." The Confederacy pledged to pay the tribes' annuities. The Chickasaw and Choctaw in turn promised to raise a regiment of mounted soldiers to battle Union troops seeking to invade Indian Territory.

Some Chickasaw disapproved of the treaty. About 225 men, women, and children—most of whom were full-bloods—declared themselves neutral and, to escape the wrath of their Confederate-supporting kin, left the Chickasaw Nation. For most of the duration of the Civil War, the neutrals lived in Le Roy, Kansas, with like-minded refugees from the Creek, Cherokee, and Seminole nations.

The traffic of refugees also moved from north to south. By the middle of 1863, the northern half of Indian Territory had been taken by the Union army. Thousands of Cherokee, Creek, and Seminole families then fled southward, many into the Chickasaw Nation. The Chickasaw generously offered the refugees food and shelter even though provisions were in short supply. With much of the male population away fighting, the Chickasaw were barely able to plant and harvest enough food for themselves.

In February 1864, Union soldiers invaded the Chickasaw Nation itself. Led by Colonel William Phillips, the U.S. force marched as far southwest as Fort Arbuckle before returning to their base at Fort Gibson in the Cherokee Nation. During their march, Phillips's men killed more than 250 Confederate soldiers. Along the way, the colonel also distributed copies of a proclamation from President Abraham Lincoln promising amnesty to Confederate allies who abandoned their support of the South. Phillips also wrote letters offering Indian leaders "pardon and peace," including one to the Chickasaw governor Winchester Colbert that warned that the tribe's "day of grace would soon be over."

Alarmed by the invasion, several Confederate-allied tribes of Indian Territory met at a council at Tishomingo in the Chickasaw Nation to discuss whether or not they should shift their allegiance. The Cherokee, Creek, Seminole, Osage, and Caddo representatives favored siding with the Union. Only the Chickasaw and the Choctaw wanted to remain true to the Confederacy. In the end, they convinced the other tribes to continue to support the South.

In April 1865, the Confederacy gave up the fight and surrendered to the United States. The Confederate tribes of Indian Territory were terrified of what might happen next. Many Indians

were convinced that they would be forced by the U.S. peace treaty commissioners to cede land in punishment for their treason. At two intertribal councils, these tribes pledged to band together and, as a group, refuse any U.S. demands for Indian land.

In late June 1865, Union commissioners arrived in Indian Territory to sign truces with the Confederate-allied tribes. Represented by Governor Colbert, the Chickasaw Nation on July 14 became the last group to surrender. A month later, delegates from the defeated tribes were summoned to Fort Smith to negotiate their peace treaties. Commissioner Dennis W. Cooley opened the council by stating that the Indians who had signed treaties with the South had "forfeited and lost all their rights to annuities and lands. The President, however, does not desire to take advantage of or enforce the penalties for the unwise actions of these nations." Even with this offer to compromise, the delegates were so resistant to hearing the federal government's demands that Cooley disbanded the huge council and decided instead to meet with tribes individually.

The exceptions to Cooley's plan were the Chickasaw and the Choctaw, with whom the United States wanted to make a single agreement because of their joint ownership of the Leased District. In April 1866, the two tribes sent delegations to Washington, D.C., to meet with commissioners. In the treaty the tribes negotiated, they agreed to

Cyrus Harris, who was elected the first governor of the Chickasaw Nation in 1856.

Chickasaw governor Winchester Colbert was the last leader of a Confederate-allied Indian tribe to surrender to the United States following the Civil War.

abolish slavery in their nations, to allow two railroads—one running north to south and one running east to west—to be built through their territory, and to participate in an intertribal council to discuss the possibility of forming one government for all the tribes living in Indian Territory. The neutral Chickasaw and Choctaw refugees would receive $260,000 from the national tribal funds in compensation for their suffering during the Civil War.

Unhappily, the Chickasaw and the Choctaw also ceded the Leased District to the U.S. government. The United States put aside $300,000 for payment for this land but would give it to the tribe only after they had made citizens of all the freed black slaves, or freedmen, in their nations. Freedmen also were to receive 40 acres of tribal land or $100 from the $300,000 fund if they chose to leave the Chickasaw and Choctaw nations. If the tribes did not grant their freedmen citizenship and land within two years, the United States had the right to use the fund to remove freedmen to a new home.

Although the penalties the United States inflicted on the Chickasaw were much milder than those imposed on the seceding Southern states, the war left the Chickasaw Nation in turmoil. The economic and cultural institutions they had worked so hard to establish after removal now had to be rebuilt. The war had also reminded the Chickasaw of the power of the United States. As they labored to reconstruct the Chickasaw Nation in the years to come, this power would seem even more than ever a threat to their very being. ▲

A late-19th-century photograph of Capitol Avenue in Tishomingo, the capital of the Chickasaw Nation.

THE
BATTLE
AGAINST ALLOTMENT

Although the Civil War left portions of Indian Territory a wasteland, the Chickasaw Nation was relatively unscathed. With the exception of the brief invasion of Colonel Phillips's Union forces, no major military campaigns had been staged within the tribe's boundaries. But all aspects of the Indians' lives had been affected by the war. The Chickasaw ecomomy was a shambles. During the conflict, businesses had been closed, fields had been left untended, and livestock herds had been raided by hungry soldiers and refugees. Lacking funds, the tribal government had barely functioned. The tribal courts had stopped operating, and the national council had met irregularly, leaving the Chickasaw governor with more power than he was author-ized to hold by the tribe's constitution. The Chickasaw schools had also closed so that the buildings could be used as barracks and hospitals.

Much of the responsibility for rebuilding what the Chickasaw had lost fell to the tribal government headed by Cyrus Harris, who was reelected governor in 1866. Its first goal was rebuilding the Chickasaw Nation's school system. Using the first annuities received from the U.S. government in 6 years, the tribe reopened 11 schools in 1867. Education continued to be a priority, and in the 1870s many new schools were built. The Chickasaw's renewed commitment to education was so strong that by 1880 more than half of the tribal population was able to read and write in English.

84   THE CHICKASAW

Missionaries slowly resumed their work among the Chickasaw. In the first decades after the war, the Methodist Episcopal church had the most influence with the tribe. But in the early 1870s, Baptist preachers began to compete with the Methodists for Chickasaw congregations. In one 3-year period, the Baptists constructed 20 churches in the Chickasaw Nation.

In the postwar era, farming continued to be the Chickasaw's most important economic activity. Their rich land brought a maximum yield from a minimum amount of labor, and both large plantations and small family plots flourished. But the Chickasaw economy was changing. In the late 19th century, Indian Territory represented one of America's last frontiers. Just as non-In-

Chickasaw and non-Indian settlers gathered to celebrate the arrival of the first train in Tishomingo in 1902. Railroads brought so many whites into the Chickasaw Nation that by the end of the 19th century, non-Indians outnumbered the Indians living on the tribe's lands.

dians had been eager to settle the Chickasaw land in Mississippi in the early 19th century, white settlers now set their sights on the tribe's western territory. The mixed-bloods were generally willing to cooperate with land-hungry whites, possibly only to make a quick profit from tribal resources but perhaps also because they felt that the non-Indians' invasion of their lands was inevitable.

Railroads were largely responsible for bringing non-Indians into the Chickasaw Nation. The first railway through their lands was the M.K. & T., also known as the Katy. Completed in 1872, the Katy crossed the southeastern corner of the Chickasaw Nation. In 1887, construction ended on a second line, the Sante Fe Railway. The Sante Fe ran north-south, from the Canadian River to Texas. The final decades of the century witnessed the completion of a number of other, smaller lines that eventually crisscrossed the entire Chickasaw Nation.

As the railways were constructed, towns quickly grew up adjacent to them. The towns' populations were made up largely of white businessmen, craftsmen, laborers, railroad workers, and shopkeepers. In time, these towns increased in size and wealth, and the inhabitants came to resent tribal control of the land on which their homes and businesses were built. With the permission of tribal officials, non-Indians could use Chickasaw land, but because the land's title belonged to the Chick-

asaw people, whites could not own tracts in the Chickasaw Nation. Whites were also angered that they had to obtain noncitizen permits from the tribe in order to live or work within the nation's boundaries. Over time, the cost of the permits fluctuated from a nominal 25 cents to a substantial $25.

Although the Chickasaw did not believe in private land ownership, tribal law gave individual tribal members the right to select a tract of unoccupied land to use as they wished. Many mixed-bloods saw in this law the opportunity to make a fortune. They claimed huge tracts along the Red, Washita, and Blue rivers and rented portions of the fertile lands to white settlers with noncitizen permits. The mixed-bloods became wealthy, and the tenants became angry as they watched the landlords grow rich from their labor.

Enterprising Chickasaw also took advantage of the increasing traffic of Texas cattlemen driving their herds through tribal lands en route to markets in Kansas. Claiming land along cattle trails, these Indians leased to the cattlemen pastures in which their herds could graze. The Texans were also required to pay to the Chickasaw government an annual tax of 25 cents for every animal grazing on tribal grassland.

At this time, there also came from Texas an influx of freedmen hoping to escape the hostility of whites in the South. Destitute and starving, the blacks often stole Chickasaw livestock and crops in order to survive. The

An 1885 photograph of a store owned by William L. Byrd, who served as the Chickasaw governor from 1888 to 1892.

Chickasaw asked the federal government to expel the immigrants, but their requests had little effect. The Indians resorted to organizing vigilante patrols to hunt down and punish the newly arrived freedmen with whippings. The Chickasaw's actions brought severe criticism from federal officials investigating charges of the Indians' mistreatment of blacks in their nation.

The prejudice suffered by the Texas freedmen grew from the Chickasaw's fear that an increase of the number of blacks in their territory would erode tribal power. Since 1866, the tribe had repeatedly asked the U.S. government to remove their freedmen to the Leased District, which the tribe had ceded to the government in the peace treaty signed by the Chickasaw in that year. The Chickasaw rejected the United States's offer to pay them $300,000 if they integrated the blacks into their tribe, partly because, as citizens, the freedmen would be entitled to a share of the tribal annuities. The federal government chose to ignore the problem, making no plans for the blacks' removal and also retaining the $300,000 fund. The Chickasaw were afraid the United States planned eventually to force them not only to take their freed slaves but also the recent black immigrants into the tribe.

The large number of whites coming to the Chickasaw Nation also alarmed the tribe. The Indians saw that they were rapidly becoming a minority in their own land. As the non-Indian population grew, they put increasing pressure on the U.S. government to open up the Chickasaw Nation for settlement so that non-Indians could own their land rather than rent it from the Chickasaw. In fact, whites throughout the West were clamoring for title to tribal lands.

Congress responded in 1887 by passing the General Allotment Act, also known as the Dawes Act after the legislation's greatest advocate, Senator Henry L. Dawes of Massachusetts. The act authorized the president to break up tribally owned lands into allotments that would then be parceled out to individual tribal members. Allotments would become the private property of their Indian owners and could not be sold for a period of 25 years. If there was tribal land left over after each tribal member eligible for an allotment received a plot, the surplus land could be sold to non-Indians. The Dawes Act also stipulated that all allottees would automatically become U.S. citizens, a

first step toward dissolving tribal governments.

In a matter of years after the passage of the Dawes Act, control of millions of acres of land throughout the United States passed from the hands of Indians into those of whites. The powerful Five Civilized Tribes were exempted from the Dawes Act, but tribes in western Indian Territory, including the Leased District, were not. As these lands were allotted, white settlers rushed in to purchase the surplus territory or sometimes to obtain title to allotments illegally. In 1890, the federal government organized the western half of Indian Territory as Oklahoma Territory, an action that brought even more non-Indians to the region. Wanting more land, these newcomers agitated for the allotment of the rest of Indian Territory.

In 1893, the federal government formed a special commission of negotiators to achieve this end. Named the Dawes Commission, this group of federal representatives was to negotiate treaties that would lay out terms for the allotment of the land held by the Five Civilized Tribes. When the commissioners arrived in Indian Territory, they found that the Indian leaders they met with were courteous but unwilling even to discuss allotment. The tribes in what remained of Indian Territory were well aware that allotment had meant the loss of an enormous amount of land to their western neighbors.

The Dawes Commission's reception did nothing to lessen the determination

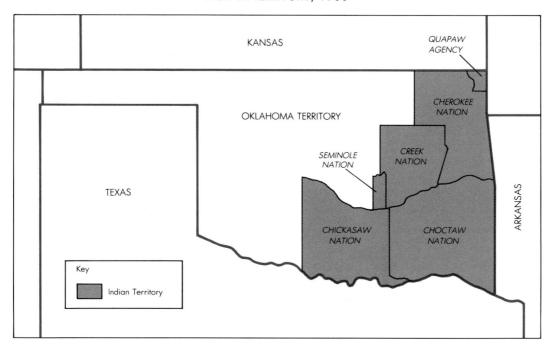

of the United States to allot Indian Territory. In 1895, Congress appropriated $200,000 for surveying the territory of the Five Civilized Tribes in preparation for division of the tribal nations. In the same year, it granted the Dawes Commission the right to compile tribal rolls that would list the name of everyone in each tribe who was to receive an allotment of land. This law was especially upsetting to the Indians, for it gave the commissioners the power to give allotments to whomever they chose without any input from tribal leaders.

The Choctaw agreed to speak with the Dawes Commission. They hoped that their cooperation would persuade the commissioners to give them some voice in determining who would be eligible for the allotments. Past treaties provided that the Choctaw could not negotiate the transfer of their land without the Chickasaw, but the Chickasaw still refused to discuss the subject of allotment. In 1896, the Dawes Commission negotiated an allotment agreement with the Choctaw, anyway. The Chickasaw were incensed and sent a delegation to Washington, D.C., that persuaded officials to disregard the illegal treaty.

The next year, Congress adopted a series of laws that were designed to reduce severely the power of tribal governments. This action finally made the Chickasaw believe that they had no choice but to talk with the Dawes Commission. Reluctantly, representatives of the tribe traveled to Atoka in the Choctaw Nation, where, with a Choctaw delegation and the commissioners, they negotiated an allotment agreement.

The Atoka Agreement had to be approved by both the tribal government and the Chickasaw people before it could be ratified by Congress. The tribal government accepted its terms, but Chickasaw voters rejected the agreement. This ruling was not accepted by the United States, however. In June 1898, Congress passed the Curtis Act, which consolidated previous laws aimed at dissolving tribal governments. It also required that the Atoka Agreement be resubmitted to Chickasaw voters. With a few minor amendments, the agreement was finally approved by the Chickasaw two months later.

According to the Atoka Agreement, "all the lands within the Indian territory

Freedmen applying for allotments of land in the Chickasaw Nation, photographed in the first decade of the 20th century. The roll of freedmen entitled to 40-acre plots eventually included almost 5,000 names.

belonging to the Choctaw and Chickasaw Indians shall be allotted to the members of said tribes so far as possible a fair and equal share thereof, considering the character and fertility of the soil and the locality and value of the lands." The document further stated that freedmen and their descendants would each receive 40 acres of land. No allotment could be sold or taxed for 25 years. Exempted from allotment were mineral reserves and all land occupied by towns and public buildings. The Atoka Agreement called for the town sites to be sold, with the proceeds to be distributed among the enrolled Indians; a 1902 amendment provided for the same course to be taken in disposing of the tribes' mineral reserves. The Choctaw and Chickasaw governments were to terminate on March 4, 1906.

The first step in carrying out the allotment of the Chickasaw Nation was to complete the tribal roll. To oversee the enrollment process, the Chickasaw formed the four-member Chickasaw Citizenship Commission, which included one representative from each of the counties in the Chickasaw Nation. The Chickasaw Citizenship Commission complained that many of the people the Dawes Commission was including on the official roll were not tribal members, but the commissioners ignored their protests. The Chickasaw then appealed to Congress, which created the Choctaw-Chickasaw Citizenship Court, made up of three federal officials, to rule on the eligibility of the

allotment applicants contested by the Chickasaw. Of the 3,679 applicants in question, the court rejected all but 156.

On January 1, 1906, the Chickasaw tribal roll was finally completed. It listed 1,538 full-bloods, 4,146 mixed-bloods, and 635 whites married to Chickasaw individuals, each of whom was entitled to an allotment of approximately 320 acres. The roll of freedmen who would receive 40-acre plots contained 4,670 names. Between 1903 and 1910, the enrolled Chickasaw and freedmen chose their tracts.

Although the Chickasaw government was not officially dissolved until March 1906, the tribal leaders had essentially lost their power a good deal earlier through the provisions of the Curtis Act. However, in 1905 the tribal government did join with leaders from the other Five Civilized Tribes to protest a congressional plan to merge Indian Territory and Oklahoma Territory to create a new state to be called Oklahoma. The Indian leaders petitioned the federal government to create a state from Indian Territory alone. They proposed that it be named Sequoyah after the Indian leader who invented the Cherokee alphabet. The Sequoyah Movement failed, however, and Indian Territory and Oklahoma Territory entered the Union as the state of Oklahoma on November 16, 1907.

The Chickasaw had had to fight to retain their traditions ever since they first encountered non-Indians. By the late 19th century, few of their old ways

The members of the last legislature of the Chickasaw Nation in 1906, the year the tribal government was dissolved.

were followed or even known. The two most important features of traditional Chickasaw life that still existed were a representative tribal government and the practice of holding their land in common—the two very things that the U.S. government sought to destroy in the last years of the century. With its integration into Oklahoma, the Chickasaw Nation ceased to be. And as the 20th century began, the Chickasaw people found themselves, whether they liked it or not, citizens of the nation that had obliterated their own. ▲

The Chickasaw capitol building in Tishomingo, photographed in about 1900. In 1989, the Chickasaw purchased the massive structure from the state of Oklahoma. Planning to convert the building into a tribal cultural center, the Chickasaw today see the old capitol as a symbol of their commitment to preserving their history and tradition.

THE
CHICKASAW NATION
REBORN

Many 19th-century advocates of the U.S. government's allotment policy believed its implementation would allow the Indians to hold on to the little land they still retained. Allotment supporters reasoned that, with legal title to their tracts, allottees would be safe from the onslaught of non-Indian settlers. The advocates also assumed that the government's restrictions on the sale of allotments would guarantee that the tracts would stay under the control of their Indian owners.

By the early 20th century, it was clear that the champions of allotment had been wrong. They had underestimated the greed and ruthlessness of land-hungry whites. And they had overestimated the government's commitment to fulfilling the promises it had made to Indian groups during the allotment process.

After Oklahoma became a state in 1907, many Chickasaw allottees quickly lost control of their land. Those without much experience in dealing with whites were recognized as easy prey by swindlers, who used several methods to obtain allotments. Some simply persuaded Indians to lease them land at extremely low rates. Others had themselves named as guardians of minors who had inherited allotments or of Indians judged incompetent to handle their own affairs. The most notorious swindlers convinced allottees to make out wills naming them as beneficiaries. All too often, these Chickasaw would then suddenly "disappear," leaving the beneficiaries in possession of the allotments.

But the federal government was largely responsible for the dispossession of Chickasaw landowners. Bowing to pressure from Oklahoma officials, Congress in 1908 removed all restrictions on the sale of Chickasaw allotments by blacks and mixed-bloods with less than one-half Indian ancestry. Chickasaw with between one-half and three-quarters Indian blood were permitted to sell half of their allotment. Confused and impoverished, many of these allottees were duped into selling their land, often at prices well below what it was actually worth. In 1928 and 1932, Congress acknowledged the error of lifting the restrictions on Chickasaw allotments by extending the restrictions on land owned by full-bloods for an additional 25 years. But the action came too late to have much positive effect; most of the Chickasaw allottees had long since lost their land.

Although the United States was all too eager to violate the Atoka Agreement by allowing land privately owned by Chickasaw to be sold, the government moved slowly in fulfilling its obligation to sell the 3 million acres of tribal land that was not allotted. Only after being prodded by Chickasaw leaders did the federal government actively seek buyers. The last of the Chickasaw town sites were finally sold in 1915. The government found purchasers for all of the tribal timberland in 1916 and sold the rights to the Chickasaw's coal and asphalt reserves in 1918.

The proceeds from all these sales amounted to more than $19 million, which according to the Atoka Agreement was to be shared equally by all enrolled tribal members. Just as thousands of people earlier had falsely claimed to be Chickasaw in hopes of obtaining an allotment from their territory, many non-Indians now tried to be included on the tribal roll in order to obtain a portion of the tribe's land sale proceeds. Only the protests of prominent Chickasaw individuals prevented the United States from allowing non-Indians to add their names to the roll. Between 1916 and 1925, each Chickasaw who was enrolled received approximately $1,075.

Although these payments seemed like a windfall to many Chickasaw, the money did little to relieve the poverty into which the tribe had sunk during the years following the allotment of Indian Territory. A few tribal members became rich after oil was discovered on their allotments, but the majority of the Chickasaw were extremely poor. Dispossessed of their land and discriminated against by local whites, many were unable to make a living. Their lot grew even worse during the 1930s, when the United States's economy plunged into a depression.

Recognizing the need to help Indian tribes across the country, Commissioner of Indian Affairs John Collier conceived of many innovative social and economic programs to be administered by the BIA. The Chickasaw profited from some of these. Some tribal members borrowed funds from the Indian Credit Association to start farming or poultry-raising operations. Through

Douglas Johnson, the Chickasaw governor from 1908 to 1939. Although appointed by the president of the United States, Johnson used his position to launch a series of lawsuits against the federal government regarding unfulfilled treaty promises.

the Oklahoma Indian Welfare Act of 1936, a number of young Chickasaw obtained government loans for college. The BIA also provided emergency aid to the tribe when a drought struck Oklahoma in 1936. BIA employees enabled the Chickasaw to weather the disaster by helping them can vegetables and grow crops.

The tribe's economic problems were also of great concern to Chickasaw governor Douglas H. Johnson, who served in this post from 1908 to 1939. After the Chickasaw government was dissolved, the president of the United States was given the duty of selecting an official tribal spokesman, who was referred to as the Chickasaw governor. Although Douglas was such a presidential appointee, he did not fear the federal government. One of Johnson's priorities during his governorship was to initiate on behalf of the Chickasaw a number of lawsuits against the U.S. government, many of which were concluded during the administration of Johnson's successor, Floyd E. Maytubby. Two of the most important cases involved the tribe's still unsold mineral reserves and the tract of land known as the Leased District, to which the Chickasaw and Choctaw had shared title in the mid-19th century.

The Chickasaw had long complained that the United States had not fulfilled its treaty promise to sell all of the tribe's profitable coal and asphalt lands. In 1949, Congress agreed to purchase the reserves for $8.5 million, but the Chickasaw did not see the matter as settled. The tribe and its attorneys brought suit against the government the next year, seeking additional compensation. The Indian Claims Commission (ICC), a special tribunal organized in 1946 to hear Indian groups' complaints against the United States, ruled in favor of the Chickasaw and ordered the federal government to pay the tribe an award of $3,489,843.

The Leased District dispute dated from 1866, when the Chickasaw and the Choctaw agreed to cede this area in southwestern Indian Territory to the U.S. government. According to the Treaty of 1866, the government would pay the tribes $300,000 for this land if they incorporated their freed slaves into their nations; if the tribes refused, the money was to be used to remove the blacks to the Leased District. In the years that followed, the Chickasaw declined to grant citizenship to their freedmen, but the United States did not remove the blacks. In 1951, the Chickasaw and the Choctaw stated before the ICC that the federal government violated the 1866 treaty because it did not spend the $300,000 fund either by giving it to the Chickasaw or by financing the freedmen's removal. In compensation, the tribes were awarded $902,008, one-fourth of which went to the Chickasaw.

As the Chickasaw were celebrating their court victories, the U.S. government was developing a new policy known as termination. In order to save federal funds, the United States made plans eventually to dissolve the economic ties the federal government had to many Indians according to the provisions of past treaties. For instance, the government wanted to cease payment of annuities and to stop holding funds in trust for Indian tribes. Initially, the United States wanted to terminate only tribes that had a sufficiently thick financial cushion so that they would not suffer from an abrupt withdrawal of federal economic support. Because of their large court awards, the Chickasaw tribe appeared to be an ideal candidate.

Luckily, a bill to terminate the Chickasaw and the other Five Civilized Tribes was not drafted until 1958. By

The inauguration of Chickasaw governor Overton James in October 1963. During his administration, the annual revenues of the Chickasaw government increased almost tenfold.

that time, termination was being viewed dimly by many members of Congress. For most of the tribes that had been terminated, the policy had proved disastrous. Rather than saving money, the U.S. government was spending more than ever before on welfare for terminated Indians who otherwise would have been unable to survive after they lost the treaty benefits due to them from the government. In light of this experience, Congress voted against terminating the Five Civilized Tribes.

The failure of termination also led the federal government to experiment in the 1960s and 1970s with giving Indians more input and more responsibility in their dealings with the United States. For the Chickasaw, this meant the opportunity to elect their own governor for the first time in more than 60 years. In 1971, Overton James was chosen by the Chickasaw people for the post. As a presidential appointee, he had served as governor since Maytubby's death in 1963.

The Chickasaw government made great strides during Governor James's tenure. In 1985, he explained:

> When I came into office, of course, we didn't have anything. We didn't have an office; we didn't have any employees; we didn't have any programs; we didn't have any services that were offered. And being governor at that time was more or less an honorary position. All you did was represent the tribe; you were the official representative to sign legal documents.

Despite the restrictions of the office, James succeeded early in his governorship in making some significant contributions to his people's well-being. He was instrumental in persuading the federal government to establish an Indian Housing Authority in Oklahoma. To increase the Chickasaw's awareness of issues relating to the tribe, he also organized community meetings and started a newsletter, which eventually developed into the tribal newspaper, *The Chickasaw Times*. But it was not until after Congress passed the Indian Self-Determination Act in 1975 that James could obtain enough funding from the government to make any substantial changes in the economic and social conditions of the Chickasaw. According to Bill Anoatubby, who succeeded James as governor in 1987,

> [The Chickasaw government's] budget in 1975 was about $750,000. In 1978 our budget was in excess of $5 million. So, you can see the difference in [three] years. We had 30 to 35 employees in 1975 and it went to over 200 in 1978.

The next year, the tribe approved a new constitution, which declared that the Chickasaw Nation was once again a political entity. According to the amended version of this constitution drafted in 1987, the Chickasaw government now consists of an executive, a judicial, and a legislative branch. The executive includes the governor and the lieutenant governor, both of whom are elected for a four-year term. Three judges make up the judicial branch, and 13 legislators form the legislative department. The legislature's meeting room and the offices for all tribal officials are located in the Chickasaw Nation headquarters in Ada, Oklahoma.

Since the late 1970s, the Chickasaw government has continued to grow at a steady rate. Its annual revenues are now approximately $7.5 million. The many programs funded by the Chickasaw government are designed to improve the quality of the Chickasaw people's lives today and to build a foundation for prosperity in the future.

Health care is one of the tribal government's highest priorities. The Chickasaw Nation now operates two clinics, one in Tishomingo and one in Ardmore. Among the services they provide are prenatal and postnatal care, family planning, nutritional guidance, and health education. The clinics' doctors and dentists see almost 20,000 patients annually. Nurses employed by the Public Health Nursing Program also make approximately 1,000 home visits each year. Established in 1983, this program emphasizes preventive medicine. Additionally, the tribal government provides Chickasaw Nation citizens with mental health counseling at the Carl Albert Indian Health Facility and with substance abuse treatment at the Kullihoma Alcohol/Drug Treatment Center.

Providing safe and sanitary housing to the needy is another goal of the Chickasaw Nation. Founded in 1966,

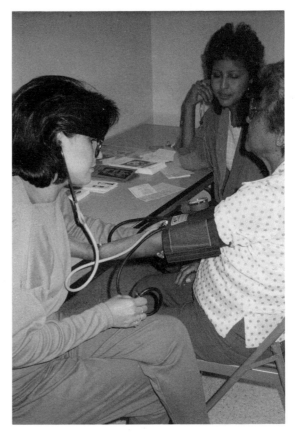

A nurse employed by the Chickasaw government checks the blood pressure of a patient. Providing quality health care for tribal members is one of the Chickasaw Nation's priorities.

the Chickasaw Housing Authority has funded the construction of almost 2,000 homes for low-income families and of Chickasaw Towers, a 9-story apartment building for the elderly. The Housing Improvement Program is designed to help families that live in overcrowded conditions but that do not qualify for other housing assistance. Other proj-

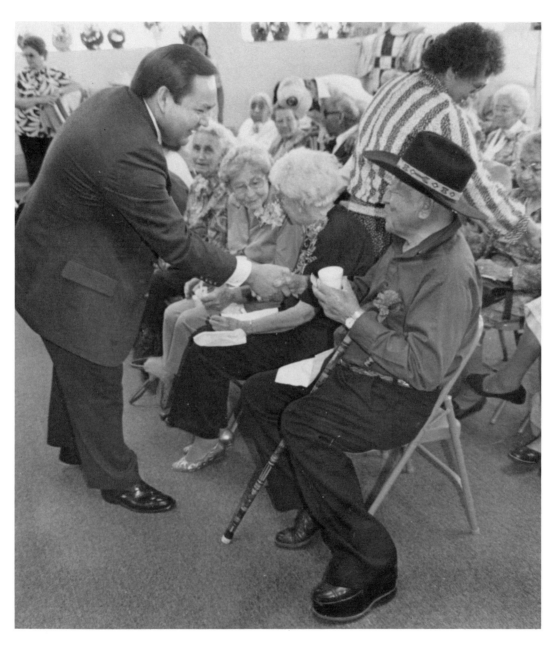

Governor Bill Anoatubby shakes hands with a tribal elder at a luncheon for senior citizens. The Chickasaw Nation's Indian Senior Citizens Program seeks to serve the social, physical, and financial needs of the tribe's elderly.

ects sponsored by the tribal government assist impoverished Chickasaw with the payment of utility bills and provide them with food and clothing.

In order to raise the Chickasaw people's standard of living, the Chickasaw Nation is working to help tribe members develop marketable job skills through classroom and on-the-job training. A summer program employs young people between the ages of 14 and 21 in nonprofit organizations throughout the Chickasaw Nation. The objective of the program is to teach the youths good work habits and to encourage them to continue their education.

The Chickasaw Nation itself employs a significant number of tribal members. In addition to administrative and clerical jobs at the tribal headquarters in Ada, Oklahoma, there are employment opportunities in the businesses run by the tribe. One of these is the Chickasaw Trading Post, which includes a convenience store and a gift shop, located in the town of Davis. The post has been so successful that the tribal government is planning to construct a second one in Ada. The Chickasaw Nation also runs the Chickasaw Smoke Shop, which sells tobacco and tobacco-related goods in Sulphur, Oklahoma; a 500-seat bingo parlor in Ada; a high-stakes bingo establishment in Goldsby and in Sulphur; and a gaming center in Thackerville. The excellent camping and fishing in the area have also led the Chickasaw Nation to de-velop a thriving tourist industry as well. To accommodate visitors, the tribe operates the Chickasaw Motor Inn, a 72-room motel and restaurant in Sulphur.

As in the past, the Chickasaw today see education as the key to their children's future. Most Chickasaw youngsters now attend public school, but through a variety of programs the tribe works to ensure that the education its children receive in and out of school attends to the special needs of Indian students. The Head Start Program is designed to prepare preschoolers for kindergarten. The Johnson O'Malley Program funds extracurricular activities, workshops, and camps for school-age students. After high school, Chickasaw can obtain grants through the tribal government to help pay tuition and other expenses at universities, colleges, and community colleges. The nation also sponsors a counseling service for students choosing a college, which provides information about institutions with special scholarship programs for American Indians. At the Chickasaw's two adult education centers, tutors help people who have dropped out of school to study for high school equivalency tests. These centers also provide adults with instruction in a variety of subjects, including basketmaking and Chickasaw history and language.

Tribal members can also learn about their heritage at the Chickasaw Community Center at the headquarters complex. The center includes a museum that displays artifacts, old photographs,

A Chickasaw preschooler experiments with paint at a Head Start class. Looking to the future, the tribal government is seeking to improve the quality of education available to all Chickasaw children.

and documents to educate visitors about the history of the Chickasaw people. It also has a 4,000-volume library relating to Indian studies and a collection of videotaped interviews with Chickasaw elders who share their memories of the tribe's past.

In the 1990s, the Chickasaw plan to create a new cultural center in the old Chickasaw capitol building. Erected in 1896, this massive structure served as the seat of the tribal government before its dissolution. The capitol then became the Johnson County courthouse until 1989, when it was purchased by the modern Chickasaw Nation.

Since its reacquisition, the capitol building has served as a symbol of the Chickasaw's determination to recapture their lost culture and heritage. Such determination has allowed the Chickasaw people to persevere during centuries of constantly changing fortune, leading them to flourish in times of prosperity and to survive in times of adversity. If the past is a guidepost for the future, the Chickasaw people in the 21st century will no doubt remain determined and proud to be part of, in Governor Overton James's words, "the unconquered and unconquerable Chickasaw Nation." ▲

BIBLIOGRAPHY

Baird, W. David. *The Chickasaw People.* Phoenix, AZ: Indian Tribal Series, 1974.

Debo, Angie. *And Still the Waters Run.* Princeton, NJ: Princeton University Press, 1940.

Foreman, Grant. *The Five Civilized Tribes.* Norman: University of Oklahoma Press, 1932.

Gibson, Arrell M. *The Chicasaws.* Norman: University of Oklahoma Press, 1971.

Littlefield, Daniel. *The Chickasaw Freedmen: A People Without a Country.* Westport, CT: Greenwood Press, 1980.

Malone, James H. *The Chickasaw Nation.* Louisville, KY: John P. Martin, 1922.

Rennie, David Alexander. *Six Rennie Men Who Came to Tishomingo.* Norman, OK: D. A. Rennie, 1979.

Swanton, John R. *The Indians of the Southeastern United States.* Washington, D. C.: Smithsonian Institution Press, 1979.

THE CHICKASAW AT A GLANCE

TRIBE   *Chickasaw*

CULTURE AREA   *Southeast*

GEOGRAPHY   *Northeastern Mississippi, northern Alabama, and western Tennessee, until removal in 1837; southern Oklahoma after removal*

LINGUISTIC FAMILY   *Muskogean*

CURRENT POPULATION   *Approximately 19,000*

FIRST CONTACT   *Hernando de Soto, Spanish, 1540*

FEDERAL STATUS   *Recognized*

GLOSSARY

Ababinili The Chickasaw sun deity who is believed to have directed the people to their southeastern homeland long ago.

agent A person appointed by the Bureau of Indian Affairs to supervise U.S. government programs on a reservation and/or in a specific region. After 1908 the title *superintendent* replaced *agent*.

agriculture Intensive cultivation of tracts of land, sometimes using draft animals and heavy plowing equipment. Agriculture requires a largely settled life.

akabatle A traditional game played during the springtime Busk Festival. The players gathered around a staff placed in the center of a court and tried to throw a ball so that it struck an effigy atop the pole.

aliktce Chickasaw healers charged with curing the sick. The Chickasaw believed that the seriously ill could only be healed by the special knowledge that the aliktce obtained from supernatural beings known as Iyaganashas.

allotment The U.S. policy applied nationwide through the General Allotment Act passed in 1887, aimed at breaking up tribally owned reservations by assigning individual farms and ranches to Indians. Allotment was intended as much to discourage traditional communal activities as to encourage private farming and assimilate Indians into mainstream American life.

annuity Compensation for land and/or resources based on terms of a treaty or other agreement between the United States and an individual tribe. Annuities consisted of goods, services, and cash given to the tribe every year for a specified period.

anthropology The study of the physical, social, and historical characteristics of human beings.

archaeology The recovery and reconstruction of human ways of life through the study of material culture (including tools, clothing, and food and human remains).

band A loosely organized group of people who are bound together by the need for food and defense, by family ties, and/or by other common interests.

breechcloth A strip of animal skin or cloth that is drawn between the legs and hung from a belt tied around the waist.

Bureau of Indian Affairs (BIA) A U.S. government agency now within the Department of the Interior. Originally intended to manage trade and other relations with Indians, the BIA today seeks to develop and implement programs that encourage Indians to manage their own affairs and to improve their educational opportunities and general social and economic well-being.

Busk Festival The Chickasaw's most important ritual, traditionally held in the spring after their corn crop ripened. Beginning with the extinguishing of the community's sacred fire, the four-day observance included two days of fasting, followed by feasting, game playing, and ceremonies.

Chickasaw Manual Labor Academy Founded in 1851, the first school to be established in the Chickasaw District.

chunkey A traditional game played during the springtime Busk Festival. The game began with a special rounded stone being tossed onto a playing court. As the stone rolled, the players threw lances at it. The winner was the person whose lance struck closest to where the stone finally came to rest.

clan A multigenerational group having a shared identity, organization, and property based on belief in descent from a common ancestor. Because clan members consider themselves closely related, marriage within a clan is strictly prohibited.

culture The learned behavior of humans; nonbiological, socially taught activities; the way of life of a group of people.

Department of the Interior U.S. government office created in 1849 to oversee the internal affairs of the United States, including government land sales, land-related legal disputes, and American Indian affairs.

dialect A regional variant of a particular language with unique elements of grammar, pronunciation, and vocabulary.

Five Civilized Tribes A group of tribes that included the Chickasaw, Choctaw, Creek, Seminole, and Cherokee. These tribes were known as "civilized" because of their adoption of many non-Indian customs.

hopoye The collective title for the two holy men who directed the Chickasaw communal rituals performed to win the favor of Ababinili and other deities.

Indian Civilization Act An act passed by Congress in 1819 that allocated $10,000 of federal money for Indian education. Missionaries were encouraged to request money from this fund and use it to open schools for Indian students.

Indian Claims Commission (ICC) A U.S. government body created by an act of Congress in 1946 to hear and rule on claims brought by Indians against the United States. These claims stem from unfulfilled treaty terms, such as nonpayment for lands sold by the Indians.

Indian Removal Act A bill passed by Congress in 1830. It authorized the president to set aside land west of the Mississippi River to which eastern tribes could be relocated, or removed. According to the terms of the act, no tribe could be removed against its will.

Indian Reorganization Act (IRA) The 1934 federal law that ended the policy of allotting plots of land to individuals and encouraged the development of reservation communities. The act also provided for the creation of autonomous tribal governments.

Indian Territory An area in the south central United States to which the U.S. government wanted to resettle Indians from other regions, especially the eastern states. In 1907, this area and Oklahoma Territory became the state of Oklahoma.

Iyaganashas Three-foot-tall supernatural beings who were said to train the *aliktce*.

Lofas Ten-foot-tall supernatural beings who, according to Chickasaw legend, hid game from hunters and caused disaster.

minko The Chickasaw word for chief. A minko was the leader of a clan.

mission A religious center founded by advocates of a particular denomination who are trying to convert nonbelievers to their faith.

picofa An important Chickasaw ceremony performed to treat a seriously ill patient.

removal policy Federal policy, initiated in 1830, that called for the sale of all Indian land in the eastern and southern United States and the migration of Indians from these areas to lands west of the Mississippi River.

reservation, reserve A tract of land retained by Indians for their own occupation and use. *Reservation* is used to describe such lands in the United States; *reserve,* in Canada.

squatters People who occupy property without a legal title.

termination Federal policy to remove Indian tribes from government supervision and Indian lands from trust status, in effect from the late 1940s through the 1960s.

territory A defined region of the United States that is not, but may become, a state. The government officials of a territory are appointed by the president, but territory residents elect their own legislature.

toli A traditional game played during the springtime Busk Festival. Toli was similar to the modern-day game of lacrosse, except that each player carried two sticks instead of one.

treaty A contract negotiated between representatives of the United States government or another national government and other sovereign nations, including Indian tribes. Treaties dealt with the cessation of military action, the surrender of political independence, the establishment of boundaries, terms of land sales, and related matters.

Treaty of Doaksville An 1837 agreement in which the Chickasaw agreed to pay the Choctaw $530,000 for the right to live in the western two-thirds of the Choctaw Nation in Indian Territory.

tribe A society consisting of several or many separate communities united by kinship, culture, language, and other social institutions including clans, religious organizations, and warrior societies.

trust The relationship between the federal government and many Indian tribes, dating from the late 19th century. Government agents managed Indians' business dealings, including land transactions and rights to national resources, because the Indians were considered legally incompetent to manage their own affairs.

INDEX

DEDICATION

I would like to dedicate this book to the memory of two of the greatest authorities on Chickasaw history—Dr. Arrell Gibson and the Honorable Haskell Paul.

I studied with Dr. Gibson at the University of Oklahoma in the 1970s and always knew him to be a gentleman and a scholar. The news of Dr. Gibson's death in November 1987 shocked his many friends across the nation. He left behind a partial manuscript for this volume; I was honored when his widow, Rosemary Gibson, asked me to complete the work.

Haskell Paul, who also died in November 1987, had been an Oklahoma district judge and had served on the Chickasaw Tribal Court. For two years, he and I worked together as members of the Chickasaw Cultural Committee. Judge Paul, too, was a gentleman, proud of his Chickasaw heritage and of the Chickasaw people.

This book was made possible in large part through the assistance of the people of the Chickasaw Nation, who allowed me to interview their elders in order to collect information on the tribe's recent past. I would especially like to thank Community Health Representatives Pat Allen and Jack John, who helped me set up the interviews; Gary Childers, Rhonda Brown, and Debbie Shelton, who helped me videotape the subjects; and all the tribal elders who shared their time and experiences with me. Unfortunately, I cannot list all their names here, but I would like to express my gratitude particularly to Hattie Pickens Stout, Ben and Elsie Alexander, Sophie Perry, Juanita Tate, and Geraldine Greenwood. Thanks go as well to my family, who had to share my time with the Chickasaw during my two years of traveling to conduct the interviews.

I am indebted to Pat Ross, tribal administrator of the Chickasaw; Overton James, who was governor of the Chickasaw at the time of my research; and Bill Anoatubby, the present governor of the Chickasaw Nation. Ted Key, Ed Brown, Dorothy Milligan, and Robert Stevenson, who served on the Chickasaw Cultural Committee with me, also have earned my admiration for their efforts to promote the preservation of Chickasaw culture. And, finally, thanks to Glenda Galvan and Sue Fathree, who have made dreams of the Chickasaw Museum and Library become reality. The library allows scholars to study many Chickasaw historical documents and will surely foster future research on the tribe.

—Duane K. Hale
Norman, Oklahoma
May 1990

PICTURE CREDITS

Alabama Department of Archives and History, Montgomery, Alabama, page 47; Archives and Manuscripts Division of the Oklahoma Historical Society, pages 38, 74, 79, 80, 82, 84, 89, 91; The Bettmann Archive, pages 25, 27, 36; Courtesy Chickasaw Nation, pages 58, 73, 95, 97, 99, 100, 102; Courtesy Chickasaw Nation, Photos by Keith Robins, cover, pages 12, 15, 17, 19, 20, 32, 50, 54, 65–72; From the Collection of the State Museum of History, Oklahoma Historical Society, Photo by L. Michael Smith, page 45; Library of Congress, pages 31, 41, 53; Mississippi State Archives, page 28; Museum of the American Indian, page 92; National Anthropological Archives, Smithsonian Institution, pages 22, 60, 63; Peachtree Collection, Louisiana State Archives, page 34; University of Oklahoma, Western History Collection, page 86.

Maps (pages 2, 43, 56, 76, 88) by Gary Tong.

DUANE K. HALE , a mixed-blood Creek by descent, is a historian and researcher for the American Indian Institute at the University of Oklahoma. After receiving his Ph.D. from Oklahoma State University, Dr. Hale taught at Navajo Community College and at the University of Minnesota. In 1981 he returned to Oklahoma, where he has worked as a consultant for many tribes. Since 1984, Dr. Hale has written several books, including three on the Delaware Indians. He has also conducted 16 workshops in historical research attended by members of approximately 200 North American tribes.

ARRELL M. GIBSON was professor of history at the University of Oklahoma until his death in 1987. In addition to numerous articles, he wrote 25 books, including *The Chickasaws, The Kickapoos: Lords of the Middle Border,* and *The Life and Death of Colonel Albert Jennings Fountain.*

FRANK W. PORTER III, general editor of INDIANS OF NORTH AMERICA, is director of the Chelsea House Foundation for American Indian Studies. He holds a B.A., M.A., and Ph.D. from the University of Maryland. He has done extensive research concerning the Indians of Maryland and Delaware and is the author of numerous articles on their history, archaeology, geography, and ethnography. He was formerly director of the Maryland Commission on Indian Affairs and American Indian Research and Resource Institute, Gettysburg, Pennsylvania, and he has received grants from the Delaware Humanities Forum, the Maryland Committee for the Humanities, the Ford Foundation, and the National Endowment for the Humanities, among others. Dr. Porter is the author of *The Bureau of Indian Affairs* in the Chelsea House KNOW YOUR GOVERNMENT series.